AF480664

Kentucky's Last Barefoot Generation

Kentucky's Last Barefoot Generation

Growing up off the Grid for Real

Paul McCarty

Printed in the United States of America

ISBN 979-8-9954619-0-6

First Edition

Published by McCarty Publishing
Beechgrove, Tennessee

In loving memory of our Mom and Dad. We wish we could turn back time to thank you for the care and sacrifice you made for each of us.
And to our brother Doug—we carry your memory with us always. We miss you every day.

Contents

1

A Time of Wonder

I was born two years before the United States entered World War II and grew up in a rural environment where children went barefoot more often than not, where the sound of a screen door slamming meant someone was either coming in to eat or headed back to the fields, and where the arrival of the fall Sears and Roebuck catalog was more exciting than Christmas morning.

We knew very little of the outside world. We focused on things that directly mattered and only knew that tobacco needed cutting, cows needed milking, and that if we wanted toys, we would have to get busy making them.

Looking back now, I realize we belonged to the last generation to grow up entirely off the grid and attend a one-room school barefoot.

In the fall of 1949, I was nine years old and living on our small farm between Eastview and Big Clifty in Hardin County, Kentucky. One warm night I lay alone in the front yard, staring up at a sky so crowded with stars it seemed they might bump into each other. I wondered what the stars really were, what held them in place, and how the moon moved across the sky so quickly without knocking all the stars loose. We didn't have electricity, so there were no electric lights to dim my view of the sky, nor a television to pull me back inside the house.

Mom was in the kitchen finishing canning a bushel of beans, but the faint glow from the coal-oil lamp she was using could in no way compete with the brilliance of the stars.

Lightning bugs flashed as they floated back and forth across the yard and the open grassy space between our house and the barn. Most stayed no more than a few feet above the ground, but a few rose higher—almost to the top of a large oak tree standing as if on guard at the edge of our yard.

A breeze blew so gently across our nearby burley tobacco patch that the long green tobacco leaves barely moved, making no noise to disturb the stillness and silence.

The only sounds were the occasional croaking of bull-frogs in our shallow pond beside the corn crib and the faint, forlorn hooting of an owl—likely perched alone on a dead limb at the edge of the woods far behind our barn.

The sky looked as if a giant bowl, with thousands of stars sprinkled all over the inside, had been placed upside down over the entire earth. I lay there unable to take my eyes off of it - in awe of its wonder and immensity.

Eventually, I zeroed in on one especially bright star and stared at it for what must have been an hour. Nearly blind from trying not to blink, I continued to watch, hoping that particular star would be the next to fall so I could see what happened at the exact moment it left its place in the sky.

Earlier that day, my older brother Billy and I had helped Dad remove suckers from the nearly full-grown tobacco plants in our tobacco patch. The suckers were growing fast after we had topped the tobacco. After scrubbing the sticky tar from our hands with plenty of lye soap, we milked our three cows, finishing just before dark. That evening, we ate a supper of cornbread, green beans, and hominy, and drank cool milk that had been chilling in the well all day.

After supper, I went outside to use the outhouse. On my way back, I looked up at the sky—clear and not a cloud in sight. The moon was beginning to set, sinking quickly toward the horizon as if trying to burrow down into the earth. It seemed so large and close that I felt I could reach out and touch it with a long stick. I thought about running toward it, to see whether it grew even larger the closer I got.

Seeing the sky so bright and clear, I decided it was the perfect night to watch for falling stars. It was a Friday, which meant I didn't have to wake up early to milk our cows and then walk the two miles with my siblings to our one-room school-house.

I had seen lots of falling stars shooting across the sky, but never one at the instant it began to fall. I wondered: when a star left the sky, did it leave a dark hole where it had been, or did another star immediately take its place? I had no idea what stars or the moon really were, but reasoned that new ones must take the fallen star's place, or else all of them would have fallen and disappeared long ago.

Back then, there was no internet, no cell phones, and no computers. My family didn't own a set of encyclopedias. The only way I could imagine finding an answer was to lie on my back, pick out one star from the thousands, and watch it as long as I could—hoping it would be the next to fall. I had tried many times before, but had always selected the wrong one.

As I watched the moon sink and the stars drift across the sky, I didn't think about it then, but everything we ate that day—from eggs and sausage at breakfast to cornbread, hominy, and milk at supper—had been raised or made by our own family. We had also cut and split the wood to heat the kitchen stove, washed with lye soap my Mom had made from hog fat, slept under quilts she had pieced, and played with slingshots and pop guns we had made ourselves.

In 1952, as a sixth grader, I still walked barefoot to a one-room schoolhouse. Our home had no electricity, no indoor plumbing, and no television. Just a short ten years later, in 1962, I had graduated from the University of Kentucky, started a family in Tennessee with my new bride, and was working on NASA space programs—including helping develop the rocket motors that would carry men to and from the very moon I had gazed at in wonder as a child.

Although those years shaped my siblings and me in positive lasting ways, I wish my parents hadn't had to struggle and worry so much. They lived with constant concerns—whether bills could be paid between tobacco crops, whether we children might be injured working with horses, or whether an incurable illness such as polio might strike. I wish they had been able to relax more, maybe even take a vacation.

I can only imagine how much easier life would have been for Mom if she'd had air conditioning in our sweltering kitchen while canning vegetables, or a microwave oven instead of having to stoke a fire to heat leftovers. Almost every time I now use a chainsaw, I think of how much work that one simple tool would have saved my dad when cutting firewood for the winter or staves to sell to the thriving bourbon industry in Bardstown, Kentucky.

Children Grew Up Fast

I am sure everyone has seen the signs at amusement parks indicating that children had to be so tall to ride the water slide. At other places, a sign may say "Children not allowed". No such signs were to be found on small farms, including ours. Any signs we had would probably have said something such as "children by the age of eight must learn to operate this equipment and drive these horses".

We didn't have chores – we had jobs. We were "hired" the day we could walk without falling into the hog trough.

We might get a promotion if we were lucky, to a job we could barely handle — like using a pitchfork to throw hay into the barn loft that was at least three times higher than our head or carrying a bucket of water that outweighed us by 50 pounds. We didn't even have to apply for the promotion. We were automatically qualified based on our shoe size.

Without automation or a tractor, everything had to be done manually, such as picking corn by hand and using wagons and pitchforks to move hay from the field to the barn loft. Life on small rural farms like ours required the entire family to work together to make ends meet. Kids were expected to grow up fast so they could provide more help on the farm. Although we sometimes thought work was all we did, we actually had plenty of time for fun and just being kids.

My brothers and I grew accustomed to working at a young age. We milked two or three cows, fed the livestock, and helped grow crops such as tobacco, corn, and hay.

We began helping out on the farm at a very young age - often as young as five years old. Even at that age, kids could help by performing simple tasks such as pulling weeds from around small plants or placing a spoonful of fertilizer near the base of the tobacco plants. Young kids could also gather the eggs, carry in kindling for building fires, feed the dogs and cats, and help pick beans in the garden.

At that age, we didn't think of it as work. It was fun - our way of showing our parents how big we were. Their bragging about how we didn't spill the fertilizer or break any of the eggs getting them out of the nest motivated us to attempt other, more complicated tasks.

At seven or eight, kids could scamper into the barn loft and use smaller pitchforks to help throw hay to the livestock or help Mom by washing jars she needed for canning vegetables.

Sometimes, though, I suspect Mom would rather not have had our help, such as when Doug, at age five or six, decided to surprise Mom by bringing in the clothes from the clothesline while she was still in the garden. He had pulled them still wet from the clothesline, then dragged them through the mud and into the house. Mom didn't notice him "helping" until after he had piled all of them on the kitchen floor with muddy footprints on at least half of them. Bragging on him for that job well done was likely somewhat muted that time.

As we grew older, we were given greater responsibilities and worked with less supervision from our parents. We drove the horses at eight or nine years old while Dad was plowing, and at ten, we could use horses by ourselves to disk and prepare the fields for planting. At twelve years old, we could harness the horses and hook them up to the equipment.

Burley tobacco was our primary cash crop, requiring lots of hands-on work from early spring to early winter. We performed all tasks from setting out the plants to stripping the cured tobacco. At an early age, we were taught to pull the correct-size plants from the tobacco bed and set them out in straight rows-.

In addition to the fieldwork, we, helped cut firewood using a two-person crosscut saw and sharp axes, picked blackberries, helped butcher hogs, carried eggs and cream to the store and sold them, took care of younger siblings while our parents worked in the fields, and helped in the large garden that provided food for the family year-round. We also assisted with canning by helping string and break beans and carrying in wood for the kitchen stove that was used during canning. In addition, we helped with smaller tasks such as chasing and catching chickens for Mom to dress and fry for dinner, threading needles, gathering walnuts, and occasionally going to neighbors to borrow or return small items such as hammers or cups of sugar.

Dad was never one to waste words. When telling us to do something, he expected us to figure out how to do it without getting hurt. When he told us to plow the tobacco, then that was usually the only instruction he gave us. He didn't tell us which horse or plow to use, which harness to put on the horse, or whether to plow in the morning or afternoon. He also didn't tell us to uncover tobacco plants and leaves we had accidentally plowed under. Those were details that he expected us to know or work out for ourselves.

Performing seemingly simple jobs, such as plowing tobacco, required more than just the ability to control the plow while driving the horse—it required balance and quick reflexes. When plowing tobacco, dirt could easily roll onto a young tobacco plant or cover some of its lower leaves. We learned early on to keep our eyes on the plants, the horse, and the plow at all times and move fast and get the dirt off the plants without having to stop the horse or lose control of the plow. As the horse kept moving, we'd hold the plow with one hand and quickly bend over and brush dirt away from a buried plant, then straighten up just as quickly to keep the plow in a straight line. It became second nature—a kind of rhythm between us, the horse, and the tobacco plants.

When our hands were full or it was too far to reach, we'd use our bare feet instead. We would use our toes to flick dirt off a leaf or uncover a plant with a quick kick or scraping motion as we walked along behind the horse and plow. The trick was to do it all without breaking stride or slowing the horse. Looking back, it's hard to believe how much coordination and dexterity it took to correctly plow the tobacco while at the same time, keep uncovering the plants. But at the time, it was just part of the day's work. I guess knocking dirt clods off the plants with our feet was a rural farm boy's version of soccer.

3

The Early Years

Anyone who has seen the movie "Grapes of Wrath" remembers seeing cars and trucks on the road loaded down with family possessions as they migrated from the Dust Bowl area to places further west, including California, looking for work.

That is close to what my Mom and Dad's car looked like as they left the mountains of Eastern Kentucky in 1939 for Northern Ohio.

They had piled as many of their possessions into the car as they could and tied the rest of them, including an old mattress, on top. A tarp, that had seen much better days, covered and protected everything except during really hard rains. In Dad's words, "It was pure hillbilly style."

There was barely enough room left inside the car for them and my brother Billy, who had been born in 1938 in Salyersville, Kentucky. Billy, at that time, was just a toddler, so they were able to find enough room for him on the rear seat by cramming him between a dishpan and their clothing. When Billy needed a nap, he would lie down in the dishpan or on the floor in front of the rear seat.

Both of my parents, Lonnie and Cora (Risner) McCarty, were born at the end of World War I and reared in the Appalachian Mountains of Eastern Kentucky near Salyersville. Both lived about 25 miles from Butcher Holler, which is now well known as the home site of Loretta Lynn. One of my uncles worked on the same shift as Loretta's dad in a Van Lear coal mine, and his family lived in company housing near the Lynn family.

My relatives, on both sides of the family, have lived in the vicinity of Salyersville ever since my fifth great-grandfather, Archibald Prater, was among the first to settle the area in 1800. Many of my relatives still reside near Salyersville.

Mom and Dad grew up in large families that worked hard, scratching out a living on small hillside farms. The great depression, World War II, and the hardships associated with rationing shaped their expectations and beliefs for the rest of their lives.

During the late 1930s, the only steady work in the mountains was in the coal mines or on the hillsides cutting timber, both being extremely dangerous. Because of the lack of nearby work, Dad and Mom decided to go to Northern Ohio, as did many others.

Traveling from Eastern Kentucky to Northern Ohio doesn't seem like such a big trip or deal today, but it was a huge life-changing decision at that time. Cars were unreliable, many roads were dirt or at best graveled, phones were nonexistent, and my parents had no assurance of finding work or housing before they exhausted their small amount of pocket money.

I don't know the details or the problems they faced along the way, but they did make it safely to Big Springs, Ohio. While in Big Springs, Dad worked temporary jobs, including as a school janitor, fireman, and barber.

I was born in early 1940, and shortly thereafter, we moved to Springfield, Ohio, where Dad got a job at International Harvester as a machine operator. While there, we lived in a second-floor apartment in downtown Springfield.

More than once, when I was two or three years old, I somehow kept finding a way out and into the street. A couple of times, street traffic actually came to a complete stop until Mom realized I was out and dragged me back inside. After that, every time Mom heard a horn blow, she would run looking for me, fearing I had somehow opened the door and had escaped again.

One time when it was extremely hot, she opened one of the windows, without a screen, to let in a little fresh air. She stepped out of the room for just a couple of minutes, and when she returned, I had climbed up on a chair near the window and was sitting on the windowsill with my legs dangling over the sidewalk 15 feet below. Apparently, that was the last straw; Mom said that she couldn't take it anymore, and she insisted that we move back to the mountains of Kentucky.

We left Springfield, Ohio, and returned to the quieter and much more rural environment of the Kentucky Mountains, away from traffic and near my maternal grandparents. My brother Doug was born soon after we returned to the mountains, giving Mom and Dad three young boys to raise.

A couple of years later, while we were living in Seitz, Kentucky, Dad was drafted into the Army. While he was away fighting in World War II, Mom struggled to watch after and take care of us three active boys.

To lessen her burden, Billy, being the oldest, went to stay temporarily with our paternal grandparents, David and Chloe McCarty, then living in Indiana.

About six months later, and while Doug was still a toddler, my maternal grandparents, Elvin and Nellie Risner, purchased a farm near White Mills in central Kentucky. When they moved to White Mills, Mom and all three of us boys went to live with them until Dad returned from the war.

Our grandparents' farm was between Highway 62 and Buckles County Road, only a couple of miles west of Four Corners. It was an ideal place for inquisitive and rambunctious young boys. We were free to play outside and roam as we wanted, as long as we stayed reasonably close to the house.

Two of my uncles were still living at home with my grandparents when we moved in.

Although I was still very young, I remember several things about our stay with my grandparents. I remember a pear tree that grew very close to the back of the house and had really soft and sweet pears. Apparently, I didn't know that fruit ripens only once a year and usually in the early fall. All spring and summer, I would keep checking to see if the tree had pears yet, and then after the pears appeared, I would check just about every day to see if they were ripe.

A drilled well was at the back of the house, and we drew water by hand using a long well bucket three or four feet long and about four inches in diameter. I clearly recall the gushing sound the water made when drained from the bucket.

I also recall being amazed at how the coal oil lamps could light up a room, and that the outhouse seemed an awfully long way from the house. Usually, I was busy playing and waited until the last possible moment to head to the outhouse. I always had to run as hard as I could, trying to avoid an accident. I can still almost feel my bare feet slapping hard against the dirt path as I was hoping I would make it in time.

Somehow, I always got there just in the nick of time, and luckily, during those emergencies, no one else was using it. I don't know what would have happened if the outhouse had been occupied. I probably would have jumped up and down, screaming for whoever was in there to hurry and get out. Most likely, I would have had an accident right there in front of the outhouse.

The Pet Sheep

My grandparents owned a few sheep, and once, a mother ewe wouldn't care for one of her newborn lambs. My grandmother brought it into the house and let it stay in a big box near the stove to keep it warm during the cold nights. She fed the baby lamb from a bottle and then let it run free and become a pet. Billy and I would play with it, and just for fun, we would encourage it to chase us and try to butt us. We would use our fists to push against its head, and we were thrilled when it learned to butt us.

As it grew older, larger, and stronger, the butting became real and rougher and eventually no longer fun, at least not for Billy and me. When it was nearly a year old, we had to watch out to make sure it was not near the house as we went outside. If it saw us, it would chase us and keep trying to butt us, just as we had trained it to do.

My grandmother continued to watch after the nearly grown sheep, still thinking of it as her pet. She would tell us that it wasn't really trying to hurt us and we should just stay away from it. But staying away from it got harder as time went on. I believe it would sometimes intentionally hang out near the door, waiting for one of us youngsters to come outside so it could play with us by knocking us down and stomping on our backs.

My grandfather saw that it was getting too rough and might actually hurt one of us. He told my grandmother they were going to have to get rid of it, but she kept resisting, apparently believing everyone was exaggerating its real behavior.

One day, my grandmother was in the garden picking beans and apparently didn't even realize the sheep was nearby. It came up unnoticed behind her, and she suddenly found herself lying face down in the wet mud with her bucket of beans spilled all around her. Every time she tried to get up, the sheep would try to knock her back down. It finally tired of "playing" with her and wandered off, allowing her to get up and go back to the house.

The next day, I was watching out for the sheep, but to my relief, I didn't encounter it. A day or so after that, we had mutton for the first time.

At the time, I didn't grasp the connection between the sheep disappearing and the good-tasting mutton. I likely didn't even know what mutton was. Now, though, I strongly suspect the sheep paid a heavy price for butting the wrong person at the wrong time.

The Wild Groundhog

A water spring was located in a sunken shaded area about 200 feet behind the house. A small walk-in enclosure was built over the spring, and the cool spring water kept the inside of the enclosure cool even on the hottest of days. During the hot days of summer, my grandparents kept some foods, including milk and butter, in the water so they would stay cool and fresh.

A path leading to the spring was twisting and well-worn, but the sides were overgrown with tall weeds higher than my head.

One day, I was really thirsty and decided to go to the spring for a drink of cool water rather than going into the house for water as I usually did. I was on the path and almost to the spring when I met a huge groundhog coming toward me. He looked as big as a mountain lion, but that may have been, at least partially, because I was so small. That scene is burned into my memory so vividly that I believe I can still count the hairs on his nose.

We were within two or three feet of each other before each noticed the other. The tall, thick weeds blocked both of us from leaving the path, so neither of us moved, but just kept holding our ground and staring at each other.

I began wondering whether groundhogs would bite, or, given the chance, possibly even eat me. After what seemed like hours, I started breathing again and decided this was no time to argue about who had the right of way or who should back up. I did a quick U-turn and got out of there fast. I have no idea if the groundhog kept on his way or also beat a hasty retreat as soon as I left.

After telling everyone, several times, about my great escape, my imagination had grown the groundhog to the size of a full-grown lion. The more times I told the story, the braver I remember being when facing the groundhog. Eventually, I recalled picking up a stick and using it as a sword, forcing the

groundhog all the way back to his den. My quick action probably saved my life and the lives of everyone in our family.

However, in the real world, my bravery quickly faded,
and I never again went to the spring by myself.

My granddad's farm had red, clay-like dirt that was really
sticky when wet, and would be extremely hard to get off my
feet. But it grew big blackberries. I would find a few briars
along a fence row. Within a few minutes, I would have eaten
as many as I could and had blackberry juice all over my hands
and face. It would take two or three days for the stain to wear
off.

I started first grade at Lynnvale School while we lived in
White Mills. I walked with Billy and my uncle about a half-
mile down the lane from my Granddad's house to catch the
school bus on Buckles County Road.

Buckles Road is where my uncle, a few years older than
Billy, taught him how to play hooky from school. I was sick
and not with them on the particular day they decided to give it
a try.

While waiting for the bus, my uncle suggested they skip
school that day and just have fun. Being much younger than
our uncle, that sounded like a good idea to Billy. While my
uncle and Billy were debating the wisdom of doing that, they
heard the bus coming up the road.

Both of them, without another word, and apparently without another thought from either of them, jumped inside a large
culvert that passed under the road near the school bus stop.
They held their breath as the bus rolled over them and stopped
a few feet farther down the road, where they normally caught

the bus. The bus waited for about a minute, but the driver determined they weren't coming and left.

They stayed in the culvert until the bus was completely out of sight and then began wondering what to do next. Apparently, my uncle's planning had identified only one action - jump into the culvert. But, he then realized they couldn't just go back home because they would be in trouble for purposely skipping school.

My uncle then recommended they make up a story that they had stopped to help someone get a cow back in the field, causing them to be late and miss the bus. I suppose he figured that since they would have done a good deed, then missing the bus would be ok and maybe even regarded as a commendable action. I really don't remember if Mom and my grandmother temporarily bought the story or not. Probably not.

For some reason, Billy spilled the beans and told Mom and my grandparents that my uncle was to blame because he was the one who first suggested they skip school. Billy may have confessed because he was put under a light, or more likely, he was mad at our uncle and figured he could get the heat off himself, while getting even with his uncle. I don't know if they were punished for skipping school or let off with just a warning.

Dad came home from the war in December 1945, after having fought the Japanese in the Philippines. We were still living with my grandparents, and I clearly remember that I was almost to the top of a fence, that I was climbing over to get some walnuts, when I first saw him walking up the lane with a large pack on his back.

Soon after Dad came home, we moved temporarily to a small house about a mile from my grandparents. A little later, my Grandparents moved to a farm near Big Clifty, about 10 miles away.

I especially cherish one unbelievable Christmas, which was probably the first one after Dad returned from the war. That year, we had a real Christmas tree with popcorn strings used as decorations.

I got a real store-bought Christmas present. It was a wind-up toy bulldozer with rubber tracks, and I played with that   thing for hours at a time, pretending I was clearing fields. I would let it push over small objects, pretending they were big trees and climb over small rocks, thinking of them as large boulders.

I soon broke the windup spring but that didn't matter. I filled in for the motor and pushed it around the yard and through the dirt piles.

All of us would occasionally wrestle Dad on the floor. We must have been having a good time roughhousing with him to cause me to remember those times so well.

Juanita was born while we lived in White Mills. The family still has the canceled check for $25 used to pay the doctor for attending the at-home birth.

After staying in White Mills another six months or so, we bought a small farm with a large two-story house about ten miles away, having an East View, KY address. We lived there until I was in the seventh grade and then moved to a slightly larger farm near Big Clifty, Kentucky. Those two farms are where my siblings and I grew up and had most of the experiences described in this book.

Nellie (Dykes) and Elvin Risner - My Maternal Grandparents

Lonnie and Cora (Risner) McCarty - My Parents -Early 1940s

4

Rationing During WW II

All one has to do today to get, for instance, a bag of sugar is to make a quick stop at any grocery store, pay for it, and leave. It was not that simple during World War II, even if one had the money.

Most people born in the United States since World War II have never experienced rationing and thus have never had to legally watch and limit their purchases of sugar, coffee, and many other necessities. Neither have they had to go before a rationing board and justify, for instance, why they need to buy items that needed pre-approval.

World War II raged on several continents during the first half of the 1940s, including Europe and the Pacific. The United States rationed gasoline, butter, sugar, and several other nationally restricted commodities. These products, or their production capabilities, were needed to support the war effort, making it necessary to limit use by the public in a manner as fair as possible.

The scope of rationing during the war was far greater than many people today realize. Even bicycles and new cars were rationed. No one could buy a new car unless their old one had over 40,000 miles on it or was not repairable. During that era, 40,000 miles on any car was a lot of miles.

Everyone, including kids, registered at a local Rationing Board and then received ration books containing a certain number of coupons that had to be surrendered when purchasing restricted items. Sugar was rationed to a half-pound per adult per week. One had to present and surrender the appropriate coupon to purchase the sugar.

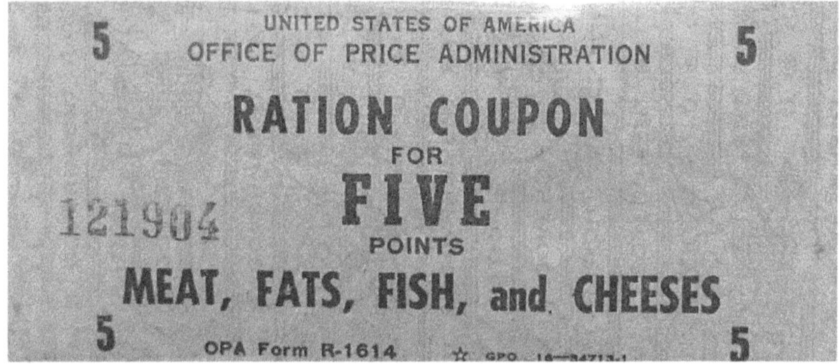

Rationing Coupon from the Early 1940s (photo from the National Museum of American History)

Rural residents were less affected by food rationing because they were able to grow their own fruit and vegetables and produce their own milk and meat. However, gasoline rationing placed a greater burden on people living in rural areas. They had to drive longer distances to purchase essentials such as flour, coffee, seeds, and fertilizers. Additionally, since most rural homes lacked electricity, they relied on kerosene (we called it coal oil) for oil lamps, which was also rationed.

Purchasing some items was much more complicated than simply surrendering a coupon. It took time to even purchase a used tire. People were allowed to own only five tires—four on the car, and one spare. Any extra tires you owned had to be turned in. Buying a new or used one or even recapping an old tire required an appearance before the Rationing Board to explain why you needed it. You would likely have to explain that you were not negligent in causing or allowing it to fail, nor had you sold or traded it to someone else. If the purchase of the tire was approved, you were then issued a certificate.

Rationing of tires was particularly worrisome because tires in the 1940s were far less durable than those of today, usually having a life of only two or three years. Blowouts and flats were a common occurrence. Everyone babied their tires and went to great lengths to prevent them from being damaged or stolen.

It was a common sight to see people working on their tires, both at home and on the side of the road. All tires had tubes, and most of those had several patches. It was also a common practice to place boots in the tires to reinforce weak areas or cover cuts and large holes. Quite often, boots were made from sections of old, unrepairable tires.

A national speed limit of 35 MPH was enacted to both save gasoline and reduce tire wear. Actually, many people were afraid to exceed 35 MPH because their tires might blow out or the boots in the tires would cause severe vibration.

Rationing drove a long-term culture of not wasting anything. Kids were taught to save resources, such as going to bed early to save lamp oil and lighting lamps from the fire in the stove instead of using matches. I recall my granddad telling us at the supper table to save bread by taking a small bite of bread and a large drink of milk

Rural residents adapted to rationing by making do with what they had such as patching torn clothing, rolling their own cigarettes, and using home-made molasses as a substitute for sugar.

Although it was illegal, neighbors would trade coupons. If someone seldom drove their car and thus did not need all their gasoline coupons, they would trade some of those for sugar or maybe coffee.

Back then, kids were not picky about what they ate. If it was on the table, we gladly and readily ate it. I am reminded of that, even now, when I see a child refuse to eat a particular food, such as a hot dog or chicken.

Many times, our supper was simply cornbread and milk. That was fine with me as I loved it. I still consider a supper of hot cornbread and cold milk to be as good as it gets – even better than a steak dinner. I would have that for my supper several times a week if my wife agreed. She often asked what I wanted for supper, and I would say, "Just make me some hot cornbread." Her usual response was "I am not going to do that because I don't want people thinking that is all I cook for you."

Growing up during the Great Depression and then having to comply with rationing drove Dad's and Mom's habits of saving anything that could be reused or repurposed.

Nothing was wasted. Paper sacks were kept for school lunch bags; Flour was purchased in colorful cloth sacks and then used to make shirts; old papers were kept to use in starting fires in our stoves; rags were turned into quilts; dogs were fed table scraps; hogs were fed anything we wouldn't eat including potato peelings and the dishwater from washing dishes - we called it slop.

Outgrown clothes, if any use was left in them at all, were handed down to younger kids. Cans and jars were reused to can vegetables, and all scrap wood was chopped into kindling for starting fires.

Coffee grounds were used as fertilizer, tobacco stalks left after stripping off the leaves were spread on the tobacco patch to build up the soil, and old Sears Roebuck catalogs were always left in the outhouse for use as toilet paper.

Our saving practices while I was growing up are probably why, to this day, I will not throw anything away if there is any possibility I can fix it. That includes TVs, power tools, washing machines, and toasters. If it can't be fixed, then before throwing it away, I save all the parts such as screws, bolts, knobs, transistors, integrated circuits, washers, and bulbs. This habit usually adds clutter, and most of the parts are never used.

While most rationing ended shortly after the war, many rationed goods, such as hamburger meat and bacon, remained in short supply and were rationed until 1954 – almost 10 years after the war. Access to products improved gradually, but some shortages lasted longer.

5

Dad Fights for Our Freedom

Dad grew up in Lakeville, KY, a small rural community just outside Salyersville in Magoffin County, Kentucky. Lakeville is now widely known as the boyhood home of Larry Flynt, the publisher of the porn magazine Hustler. Dad lived near the Flynt family, and while growing up, he often hung out with Larry's dad.

The first memory I have of my dad was when I was four years old, and he was leaving for the army during World War II. My memory is of a house set upon a little hill, and I was just barely tall enough to see over the bottom window sash and down to the road. I saw my dad jump onto the running boards of a black car and hang on as it pulled away.

His leaving must have been a traumatic event to have created such a vivid and lasting memory in a four-year-old.

Dad was in the 127th Regiment, part of the 32nd Infantry Division. The 32nd Infantry Division, famously known as the "Red Arrow Division," earned its name by breaking through every enemy line it faced. In World War II, it became one of the most battle-tested divisions in the U.S. Army.

By late 1944, the division was well into the campaign to liberate the Philippines. The 127th Infantry Regiment engaged in brutal fighting all along the Villa Verde Trail, a rugged, mountainous 22-mile supply route on the island of Luzon.

This narrow winding trail became the site of one of the bloodiest and most grueling campaigns in the Pacific. American forces, including Dad, faced well-entrenched Japanese defenders hidden in fortified caves and dense jungle.

The fighting was continuous and lasted for nearly four months against a fanatical enemy that had chosen to die rather than surrender. Around 10,000 Japanese and over 4,000 Americans, a third of the 32nd Division, were killed and countless others seriously wounded as the Americans fought their way along the hairpin turns of the Villa Verde trail high in the Caraballo Mountains.

The effort to clear the caves required extreme courage and close-quarter combat, often with flamethrowers, grenades, and explosives. Progress was measured in yards. Over a period of four months of sustained fighting, the Americans advanced inch by inch, eventually forcing a Japanese retreat and helping open the way to northern Luzon. The 32nd Division's relentless push earned it a place among the most respected units of the war—and for the men who endured the Villa Verde Trail, it left a mark that lasted a lifetime.

Information about these battles has been pieced together from newspaper articles and other sources, as Dad talked very little about his war experiences and never, if any of his kids were around.

One night, my granddad was staying with us, and I overheard Dad telling him a story about the war. One night, he and several other men were sitting around a campfire in the jungle, when all of a sudden, Japanese artillery started landing near where they were sitting. That startled him, and without thinking, he jumped up and stuck his head inside a hollow tree. He didn't have time to find his helmet in the dark and wanted to protect his head.

Each time a shell exploded nearby, rotting wood and bark would shatter and rain down on his head and neck. Sometimes, even years later, he could still feel the tree and ground shaking and the debris falling on him.

As I grew older, I was all ears every time I heard anyone mention Dad's war experiences. I know he drove an ammunition truck, took part in clearing the Japanese out of caves in the Philippines, was in multiple fierce battles, and caught malaria from being in the jungles.

I now regret not sitting down with Dad at some point after I grew up and insisting he tell me about his war experiences.

When Dad came back home, he brought several Japanese military items – a rifle, a pistol, a bugle, a sword, and sacks of rifle ammunition. I am not sure why he went to the trouble of bringing those cumbersome items all the way from the South Pacific and through Japan. He allowed us to play with them outside, and ultimately, destroy or lose all except the sword.

Times have certainly changed. As a seventh grader, I took the pistol with me on the school bus and to class, showing it around to everyone, including teachers. I seem to remember one teacher reminding me to make sure it wasn't loaded.

Wherever we lived, Dad was highly respected throughout the community, as he always tried to do the right thing and never refused to help anyone in need. He raised us kids the same way. I think that is why if we received a whipping at school, we could count on another when we got home. He never allowed us to badmouth anyone, especially our teachers.

Dad was the recognized authority figure in our family, though he was less likely than Mom to punish us for our misdeeds. Mom would often use the threat of a whipping to make us obey. If we were playing outside in the rain, she might call us in a couple of times before warning that if we didn't come in immediately, we'd get a whipping. However, we knew she only resorted to actual whippings for serious offenses, so we often tested her patience. When she resorted to the next level—threatening to tell Dad, we knew she was getting mad and we probably better listen.

Though we doubted Dad would punish us over something so small, that final warning usually got our attention and drove us into the house.

Dad's war experiences and reluctance to talk about them affected his communication with us boys as we grew up. For instance, we would work together all day without exchanging more than a dozen words, and then only if necessary to be safe and get the job done.

Of course, this could have been at least partly due to DNA. I know it carried over to my older brother Billy, as one almost had to beat a word out of him. I remember my granddad saying that if Billy was coming over to his house and passed a dead man lying in the road, he probably wouldn't even mention it.

When Dad came back from the war, he had back trouble the rest of his life. He could work hard all day long, lifting heavy things such as blocks of firewood with no problem. Then, he might simply bend over to pick up a pencil, and something would happen to his back, and he could barely move for days because of the pain. While recovering, he would often sleep on the hard floor, as it actually felt better on his back. At least once, he had surgery on his back at Veterans Hospital in Louisville, but it didn't seem to help a lot.

Later, Dad began working for Tyler Construction Company in Louisville and soon became the superintendent of a street paving crew.   For years, and before interstates, he drove approximately 60 miles each way, every workday to and from Louisville, leaving home before daylight and often getting back home after dark.   Driving that far each day must have been difficult after getting up that early and working all day.   Occasionally, he was able to carpool with someone either working at the same site or nearby in Louisville.

Billy and I, and later Doug, had to pick up extra duties on the farm after Dad started working in Louisville. We took care of the livestock and were given greater responsibility for tending the tobacco and corn crops. Juanita was much younger but still was able to help out.   Even when just six or seven years old, she was able to drop tobacco plants into the tobacco setter as Billy or I used it to set out our tobacco.

Dad as a Soldier during World War II

Off-hand casual comments can sometimes have devastating impacts on youngsters. I was always afraid of the poor house. I would occasionally hear an adult say something about the poor house and how that was likely be their next address.

One day, I overheard Dad make a similar comment to someone as they were discussing the weather. Dad said, "If it doesn't rain soon on the tobacco patch, then we probably will have to start packing for the poor house". I didn't know what a poor house was, but I was pretty sure it was something to be avoided.

For weeks after those comments, I would keep changing the channel on our battery-powered radio away from my favorite shows, including the Lone Ranger, hunting for the weather forecast. I was hoping to hear that rain was on the way, so it would reduce our chances of going to the poor house. Mom or Dad would ask why I was so interested in the weather, and I would always say something like I was just curious.

One time, I went with Dad to E-town. While there, he offered to buy me a hot dog. I actually told him I wasn't hungry, so he wouldn't have to spend the money. I was afraid the cost of that hot dog might be the last straw that sent us to the poor house. He asked if I was sick, and I think I pretended to have a slight stomach problem.

Dad also never knew how another of his casual comments affected me for years. I was going somewhere with him and opened a stick of chewing gum, and tossed a small piece of the paper out of the car window. He asked, "Did you see that sign we just passed?" I had not noticed it, and could barely read at that time anyway. He said, "It was a warning to people that they would be prosecuted for littering."

For some reason, I thought the word prosecuted meant the same as electrocuted. I had heard tales of people been put to the electric chair and I wanted no part of that. Even though I asked him to, he wouldn't go back and let me find and pick up that chewing gum paper. He said they probably wouldn't bother me over something that small.

For a long time, I really couldn't understand how he could be so casual and not be worried about even a slight chance of me being electrocuted. It was years later that I learned what the sign really meant, but until then, I was a fanatic about not littering.

Dad wasn't much of a practical joker, but I remember one instance wherein he was. A bachelor friend lived in a small one-room house near where we used to live in White Mills, KY. One day, Dad and someone with him were passing through White Mills and decided to stop and visit their friend, but he wasn't home. They tried the door, and as usual, it was not locked. They went in to wait, thinking he might be back soon. While waiting, they spotted a large pot sitting on his wood-burning stove with a fully cooked, hot chicken inside. So, as a joke, or simply because the temptation was too great to pass up, they decided to eat some of the chicken while waiting.

After they had eaten the whole chicken, and the friend had not yet returned, they put all the bones back in the pot and left. I don't remember the outcome, but I can only imagine the friend coming in from the field tired, anticipating his hot chicken cooked to perfection, and finding only meatless bones.

At least once, the tables were turned on Dad. When he was working in Louisville, Dad decided to spend a night with Mom's brother, living in Jeffersonville, Indiana, just across the Ohio River. Dad had a nice pocket watch which ran just a little slow, but not enough to bother him. My uncle wanted to try his hand at adjusting it, but Dad didn't want to risk letting him work on it.

After Dad went to sleep, my uncle slipped the watch out of Dad's pants pocket and attempted to adjust it. For whatever reason, and just as Dad expected, something did go wrong, and all the little wheels and springs jumped or fell out of the watch. My uncle tried to get everything back into the watch, but had no success. About midnight, and after giving up, he scooped up as many of the little parts as he could find, and put them back into Dad's pants pocket. Again, I don't know the outcome, but it probably didn't take Dad long to figure out what had happened to his watch.

Dad and Mom used to visit us every year or two in Manchester, and most of the time Dad and I would go fishing on Woods Reservoir in my small boat. We could usually find bluegill or crappie, and most of the time, brought them home to clean and eat.

I only remember Dad going fishing one time when I was growing up, and that was soon after we moved to the two-story house in East View. Dad went with us to a creek less than two miles away. To get there, we had to go through the woods and past an abandoned house where we children had heard that someone had died, causing us to keep clear of it. But this time, we were with Dad, so we used the opportunity to get a good look at it.

Remnants of an old water mill were near the house, with part of the water wheel still in place and a few beams still lying across the small stream that had driven the mill. Large, jagged rocks were at the bottom of the stream about ten feet below the beams. As kids will do, we used to dare each other to walk across those rotting beams. Of course, after being dared, we had no choice but to walk across them, even though falling would have been disastrous. Then, not to be outdone, the rest of us would quickly do the same.

Another grown-up went fishing with us that day, and it was likely my Uncle Ervin, who lived about a half-mile from us. I remember some of this because I was the first one to catch a small sunfish, which was no more than three inches long. I was proud of it and remember exactly where I was standing on the creek bank when I caught it.

After Dad died, I created a small collage from a few of his personal items that defined his life, interests, and the times in which he lived. Items in the collage include his pocket knife, small tools, and a tobacco spear. Also included are a horseshoe depicting how he used horses to till our farm and the carpentry tools he used to build and repair our barns, corn cribs, and fences.

6

Living off the Grid for Real

Billy and I usually took turns drawing water from the well and carrying it into the house before nightfall, so Mom would have water to use as she made breakfast and started her day early the next morning.

Several times when it was my turn to get the water, I kept putting it off until it was too dark, ensuring I would have to get up early the next morning to get the water. After I went to bed, I would completely forget about it until Mom was shaking me and telling me I needed to get up and draw the water.

As I was crawling out of bed, I regretted not having done it the night before rather than waiting until the morning. To make matters worse, during winter, it was often really cold outside, and the rope would be frozen stiff and almost impossible to maneuver to the bottom of the well.

By the time I drew the water and carried it into the kitchen, my hands and fingers were numb, but they quickly warmed by the hot stove. I would again resolve to bring in water before the sun went down. That resolution lasted only until it was my turn once again to get the water.

We didn't have a name for it back then, but the way we lived in rural Kentucky through the 1940s and into the early 1950s would now be called subsistence farming and "living off the grid." The thing is, we didn't even know there was a grid —

so there was nothing to miss. Our life was normal to us, the same way it had been for generations before us.

Today, people who choose to live "off the grid" often have backup generators, solar panels, LED flashlights, and all manner of modern gear. They also have safety nets we never dreamed of — medical diagnostics, social security, insurance, and cell phones for emergencies.

In our day, there were no shopping malls, fast-food chains, chainsaws, interstate highways, school vaccinations, or self-service groceries and gas stations. Other conveniences people now consider necessities — computers, the internet, tractors, televisions, air conditioning — were equally absent from our lives.

In some ways, we were like the Walton's show on TV, and in other ways not. Like the Waltons', we had parents who really cared for us, but unlike the Walton's, we didn't have electricity, bathrooms, or many of the other material things, such as telephones and clothes washers.

We farmed with horses, planted a garden that provided most of our food, and called the doctor to the house only for serious illnesses or injury. We drank raw milk from our own cows, butchered hogs for meat, kept chickens for eggs and Sunday dinners, rendered lard, and made our own lye soap. Our wood stoves kept us warm and cooked our meals. Most of our clothing came from the Sears & Roebuck catalog, and our laundry was done outside in a washtub with a scrub board, then hung on the clothesline to dry in the sun.

We grew and harvested our own feed for the livestock and tended an acre of Burley tobacco — our main cash crop and the backbone of our yearly income.

There were no credit cards, but it was common practice for retail businesses to allow regular, trustworthy customers to charge essential goods such as groceries and farming supplies until their tobacco crop was sold in the fall. The businesses maintained hand-written records of each customer's purchases and added up the charges when the customer was ready to settle the debt. The store owners never charged interest.

It was a constant worry to our parents that something might happen, and they would not be able to pay off what they owed. The tobacco crop might fail due to lack of rain, or something else unexpected could happen, such as getting sick and being unable to properly maintain the crops and the farm. However, things usually worked out reasonably well, and as soon as we sold our tobacco crop, Dad would go around to all the stores and pay off our debts.

Occasionally, Dad would sell a calf or pigs to provide money for everyday and urgent needs such as gasoline, small tools, and medicines. For two or three years, while still farming, Dad prepared and sold wood for making barrels to the bourbon industry around Bardstown, Ky. It was hard work in those days before chainsaws and hydraulic wood splitters. I can hardly imagine how difficult it must have been for him to get a truckload ready to sell, even though we helped when we were not in school.

Billy and I would help as he cut down large white oak trees and cut them into barrel-length logs. The only way to get the tree down and cut it into the necessary lengths was to use a crosscut saw with a person holding and pulling each end of the long saw. It would take Billy and me about 20 minutes of hard work and several rest breaks to saw through and fell a large two-foot-diameter tree.

From Left: Juanita, Billy, Doug, Me

Dad's Old Cross-Cut Saw

We would then trim the limbs from the trees with an axe and again use the crosscut saw to saw the log into the required four-foot lengths.

We rolled the logs for the best cutting positions using a log-rolling tool called a "Cant Hook".

After the logs were cut to length, Dad split the logs into triangular sections about six inches wide, using axes, wedges, and a special tool called a Froe.

Almost everyone knows how difficult it is to split blocks of firewood that are generally about a foot in diameter and only a foot, or maybe 18 inches long. The blocks of wood Dad was splitting for stave wood were typically two feet in diameter and four feet long. Those were several times harder to split than regular blocks of firewood.

Splitting the logs must have been a back-breaking task, for which both Billy and I were too young to be of much help. It involved using a large ten-pound sledgehammer to drive the froe and wedges into the wood. The split wood was then loaded by hand onto a truck, hauled 40 miles to Bardstown, and sold.

For a while, we had a battery-powered radio and could listen to the news and sometimes the weather forecast. We really didn't have much confidence in the weather forecast as it seemed to be wrong more often than right. Radio batteries were expensive and typically lasted only 40 to 60 hours. We usually limited our radio use to 30 minutes or less to conserve the battery. Each time the battery ran down, we did without a radio until Dad felt comfortable spending the money for a replacement battery, which wasn't very often.

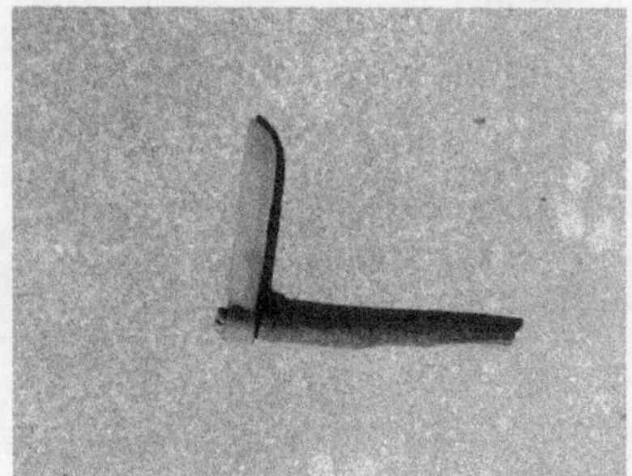

Dad's Froe (left) and Cant Hook (right)

While preparing to write this book, I started making a list of material items that are widely available today, but we did not have back in the 1940s. After two or three pages, I stopped adding to the list, as there seemed to be no end to it.

To really appreciate the material differences between then and now, all one has to do is walk around inside a big box store such as Lowes and notice how much of the inventory was not available to us during the 1940s.

Begin by realizing we didn't have any large store such as Lowes. Big box stores didn't open until the 1960s, and then only in more urban areas, not readily accessible to us. While in Lowes, first visit the tools section. Look at the rows and shelves of electric and battery-powered items, including table saws, nail guns, jigsaws, skill saws, routers, drills, impact wrenches, and electric screw drivers, which, even if available, would have been of no use to us because we had no electricity to operate or recharge power tools. Next, go to the gas-powered tools section and take notice that we had none of those labor-saving tools, including chain saws, weed eaters, lawn mowers, and leaf blowers.

Visit the lighting section and again realize that we had none of those long rows of electric lights, lamps, chandeliers, and fans. Also, we had none of the items in the plumbing, electrical, and appliances sections, including refrigerators, commodes, toasters, washing machines, microwave ovens, and dehumidifiers.

The only items in the entire Lowes store that we bought on an as-needed basis from local general stores were replacements for small hand tools such as saws, axes, hammers, and a few other essentials such as nails, fence wire, and packets of seeds.

Likewise, visit a supermarket such as Kroger's and, after walking through all the many sections and aisles, realize that the only things we bought regularly were a few items from the baking section, such as flour, black pepper, salt, and coffee. Everything else in the store, we either made, grew, or did without.

The availability of material things is not the only difference between then and now. Rural residents, such as us, would seldom lock their doors even when away from home for days. Actually, we didn't have locks on most of our doors and had lost the keys to those that did. Also, rather than trying to hide the fact that we were away from home, we would let neighbors know when and how long we planned to be gone. They would keep an eye on our livestock and feed them if needed.

There was very little crime within our local community. However, I do remember one time there was a lot of discussion about someone who had been accused of burning someone else's barn. Anyone who would do that was considered a low-life barn burner, and most everyone thought that tarring and feathering would be too good for them. Barns were critical to making a living on small rural farms. Without a barn, one couldn't house their essential tobacco crop, couldn't store hay for feeding livestock during the winter season, nor could they provide protection for the horses and cattle from the cold winter storms. Burning someone's barn, regardless of the reason, directly risks their livelihood.

Our heating system was a wood stove in the living room, where it was more or less central to the whole house. The next morning, we often found that the water in the kitchen water bucket had frozen. The thin sheet metal of the stove would heat up fast after the fire was built, but it also would cool off just as quickly as the wood burned down. It didn't take long for the entire house to get really cold once the fire had gone out. But we slept warm because we usually were covered with so many quilts we could barely turn over in bed.

During the heat of the summer, all windows, and sometimes the doors, were left open day and night so at least some of the cooler night air could enter the house. We had screens over the windows and doors to keep out flies and other insects, but there were so many holes in them that they weren't all that effective. Sometimes, when Mom was canning fruits, flies would find ways into the house in such large numbers that we would need to get them out.

We would use towels and drive the flies into one room. Someone – usually me – would then go into the closed-off room and completely fog the room using a hand-pumped Flit sprayer and fly spray. I never wore a mask while spraying the flies, and so surely inhaled a lot of the fly spray. We would

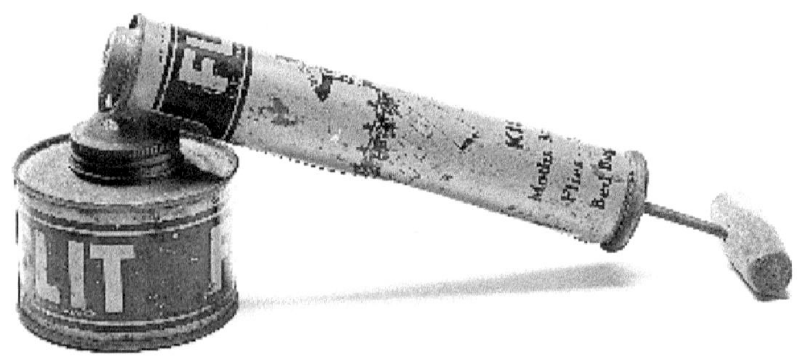

Flit Sprayer (photo from Science History Institute)

wait about 15 minutes until the flies were dead and then sweep them up and dispose of them. We would only need to spray them a couple of times each summer.

Frequently, during July and August, temperatures were really high, even at night,

Sleeping in the house became almost unbearable. That happened quite often when Mom had been canning garden vegetables on the kitchen stove and the house had become almost steamy hot. Several times, Dad and maybe a couple of us kids would spread a quilt under a tree in the front yard and try to sleep out in the open during the hottest part of the night. If there was a slight breeze, that worked out pretty well. However, on real still nights, it seemed almost as hot outside as it was inside.

Most of the time, we would only sleep there until the house had cooled down a few degrees. We then had to choose between going back into the still hot house or staying outside, where the frogs, owls, and sometimes cicadas were very loud and driving us crazy.

We didn't have a refrigerator, so when we had something that had to be kept cool, such as cream, we used a rope and lowered it into the well. The well water was not all that cold, but it was better than leaving things sitting out during hot days.

Dishes were washed by hand in a large dishpan, rinsed, and dried. The leftover greasy dishwater, which contained scraps of food, was then fed to the hogs. Chickens or the dogs would get any leftover breadcrumbs.

Our breakfast was usually biscuits and fried eggs with sausage or ham. The sausage and ham were available only during the winter months, as we had no place to store meat during the summer. We seldom had cereal, but when we did, it was corn-flakes.

Lunch was often very simple. Mom would bake a large pan of corn bread, and we would eat it with milk. If there were leftovers from supper the night before, such as mashed potatoes or green beans, then we would heat those back up and have them with the corn bread.

Supper depended on what was going on and the season. If we were really busy, for instance, stripping tobacco, we would simply have leftovers, or Mom would bake corn bread and open and heat one of her large half-gallon cans of green beans. During mid to late summer, it was usually potatoes, green beans, and tomatoes directly from the garden.

Washing days were hard, especially on Mom. Billy and I helped by drawing water from the well, carrying wood and building the fire for heating the water, and carrying clothes from and back into the house. Doug was getting old enough to help with some of the work, such as rounding up the dirty clothes to be washed.

All rural kids that I knew, including us, removed their shoes as soon as the ground began to warm in the spring, and didn't put them back on until late fall.

Within a week or two of shedding our shoes, our feet would be so tough we could easily run on gravel roads just as well as if we had shoes on. But, we were frequently stepping on nails and thorns, or dropping things on our bare feet, and limping back home with bleeding or bruised toes and feet for Mom to fix. This, along with getting sniffles and colds from going barefoot too early in the season, gave Mom ample opportunity to practice her medical skills.

7

Our Home Sites

Dad had a knack for "accidentally" putting fried chicken on the table. One afternoon, he showed up in the kitchen carrying a limp hen and told Mom, "You won't believe what happened. I stepped backward out of the corn crib without looking and stepped right on this chicken's head."

He was right about one thing—we didn't believe him for a second. Not Mom, not us kids. We all knew that the chicken's untimely end was no accident.

Fried chicken was a rare treat in our house, mostly because Mom kept putting it off due to the hours of extra work it created for her. When it did happen, the job usually started with one of us kids being told, "Go catch a chicken."

That was the fun part. Our chickens weren't penned up—they had the run of the yard and wherever they wanted to go. Catching one meant we would be jumping, zig-zagging, and trying to herd a few into a corner of a fence row or into the barn before making a wild grab or dive for a pair of legs. The ruckus always drew reinforcements - the rest of us kids and our dog eagerly joined in the chase, with all of us adding to the chaos. The dog didn't understand that we were trying to actually catch one of the chickens and seemed to believe that the point of the game was to scatter all of them each time we had a few of them cornered.

Of course, Mom had final say on our catch. If we brought her one of her prized laying hens instead of a pullet or a hen past her prime, she'd send us back out to try again. With all the dust, squawking, and flying feathers, it's a wonder any of the hens ever laid another egg.

After Mom approved the victim, she'd make quick work of it—either wringing its neck or chopping off its head using the axe. She would then spend the next hour plucking, cleaning, and cutting it up. We all looked forward to hearing the sizzling sounds as she dropped the pieces into a skillet full of hot homemade lard. The smell of frying chicken filled the whole house. Once on the table, it didn't stay there for long.

While I was in first grade at Lynnvale School, we moved about ten miles from White Mills to a 50-acre farm on Dry Ridge Road, a few miles west of Eastview. I then completed first through sixth grades at Burkhead, a one-room school roughly two miles from our house. No school buses served the area, so we walked to school, regardless of the weather.

My parents struggled to make even a subsistence living on our Eastview farm, primarily because the soil was severely depleted due to past poor farming practices or simply "worn out." Parts of the pastures were overgrown with sage grass, and the tillable fields had soil lacking in organic matter. This caused the soil to quickly lose moisture during dry weather conditions.

As a result, our Burley tobacco and corn crops were often substandard because we could not afford the large amount of fertilizer it would have taken to grow better crops. Dad tried to improve the soil by spreading tobacco stalks and manure from the barn on the fields and having lime spread on the to-bacco patch. But there were no quick fixes, as rebuilding the soil takes years if not a lifetime.

One of the hardest and maybe the dirtiest jobs we had was to spread the manure on the tobacco patch. It had to be dug out of the barn stalls using pitchforks and loaded on a wagon. We then had to spread it over the ground by hand, also using pitchforks.

Getting the manure out of the stalls was made more difficult by our habit of occasionally feeding our horses and cows hay while they were in the stalls. Some of the hay was walked on by the livestock, causing the manure to pack down into one big brick, which was hard to break up.

By today's standards, we probably would be considered poor, but we didn't realize it. Even if we had known, it wouldn't have mattered to us, as life was similar for other families in our rural area.

Although crops at our Eastview home were not as good as Dad wanted, I enjoyed living there because we were near so many interesting places to explore, and our cousins lived only a half mile from us. There was a cave on my nearby uncle's farm that we often explored, and a creek just beyond a neighbor's farm in which we fished and swam.

While I was in the seventh grade, we sold the Eastview farm and bought a slightly larger, more fertile farm, another four or five miles farther down Dry Ridge Road, to where it intersected with Solway Meeting Creek Road. Our new home was approximately three miles north of Big Clifty and had a

Big Clifty address. This farm adjoined the farm of my grandparents, who had moved from White Mills to that same location a couple of years earlier.

Our three home sites – White Mills, Eastview, and Big
Clifty were in the Southwestern section of Hardin County,
Kentucky as shown on the map.

Our Home Sites (Map from U.S. Census Bureau via Wikimedia Com-
mons)

It didn't take long for my siblings and I to discover that
our new home site would be even more fun than our Eastview
home. It had more room, including woods, within which to
roam and explore.

Meeting Creek – the creek we had enjoyed so much
while living at our East View home, actually bordered one edge
of our Big Clifty farm, and was closer to our house than before.
In addition, there were several large ditches and cliffs suitable
for climbing and exploring– absolute heaven to young boys.

A major change for me was no longer having to walk to the one-room Burkhead School. I now rode the bus back to Lynnvale School at White Mills.

This time, however, the school bus ride from our house was over an hour each way and required a transfer to another bus after reaching Western Elementary School.

The long bus trip to school gave me plenty of time to borrow someone's textbook and study for tests or pop quizzes, and even prepare homework on the way to school. Although that probably was not the best method for long-term retention of the information, it did keep me from having to take books home, and ensured the information was fresh in my head should we have a pop quiz.

About a quarter mile before reaching Lynnvale School, we had to cross the one-lane Nolin River Bridge. Two or three times a year, heavy rains would cause the Nolin River to reach flood stage with water at or above the bridge floor. It was too risky to cross the bridge in those conditions, so the bus would find a spot to turn around and go back home.

Almost everyone on the bus loved the turning around part, especially since we were in sight of the school. It was like someone handing us a "Get out of school free card". All the boys and a few of the girls always seemed in a much better mood as the bus turned around and traveled back toward home. Some of the girls actually liked school and were disappointed that they had to go back home rather than attend school.

Our Family - Mom and Dad with Me on Left; Billy in Back; Doug in Front; and Juanita in Front by Dad

Once or twice a year, the school would let out early because the river would begin rising from heavy rains. That was also exciting to us boys.

I continued attending Lynnvale School through graduation in 1958.

Our home sites in the 1940s would resemble many other small farms in central Kentucky from that era. Along with our house, there would be a barn, a few horses, cows, and hogs, and a Burley tobacco patch alongside one or two corn fields. There would also be horse-drawn implements—wagons, corn planters, hay rakes, plows, and disks—parked by the fence or scattered around the barn. Small tools such as pitchforks, hoes, and shovels were often left wherever we last used them - sometimes on the ground behind the barn. A few chairs were usually sitting under the shade trees in the front yard.

At least one or two fields would be fenced to serve as pastures for horses and cows to share. Generally, they left each other alone and remained on opposite sides of the field. Each of our farms also had a hog lot adjacent to the barn with feeding troughs positioned near the fence so we wouldn't have to enter the lot to feed the hogs.

Bicycles, or parts of bicycles, would be thrown down under a large tree in the yard. A couple of cats would be sleeping on the porch, and a dog would be close by waiting for someone to come out so it could follow them around.

Chickens were likely wandering around, scratching in the yard, searching for bugs, and occasionally jumping up on the porch and risking Mom getting a broom and chasing them off. Just about every time she did that, she would say, "Somebody is going to have to fix the door on the chicken house, and these chickens are going to stay in it". I now think that was just an expression of hers, as the chickens needed to stay outside to find most of their own food. Keeping them penned up in the chicken house would have required too much care and feed.

Nolin River Bridge during a 2024 High Water Condition

Our chickens were an absolute necessity on the farm. We normally had anywhere from 10 to 30 to ensure a supply of eggs and the occasional fried chicken dinner. Sometimes, a chicken would have a hidden nest and hatch a few chicks, but most of the time, Mom ordered chicks by mail, and we would go to the post office to pick them up. Ordering baby chickens by mail was a common practice at that time.

When we went to pick them up, it was never a problem knowing they had arrived. Thirty or 40 chicks in a box can do a lot of chirping. I suspect the post office was glad when we showed up and took them home.

Getting There

To reach our Eastview home, one would travel west on Highway 84 from Four Corners, a small crossroads community at the intersection of highways 84 and 62, near White Mills. At that time, Four Corners consisted of a grocery store, an auto repair shop, and a few homes. Not much has changed since then, except that the grocery store has been replaced with a self-service gas and convenience store.

Within a couple of miles, one would pass through Eastview, another small community with two grocery stores, a bank, and a post office. One would have to watch out for trains when passing through Eastview, as the main railroad between Louisville and Nashville passed through the center of the small community.

Continuing for another three miles, one would turn left onto graveled Dry Ridge Road. As one turned, three small grocery stores would be sited near the intersection. I am not sure whether the intersection and area even had a name, but those are the stores we primarily patronized to buy groceries and gas.

After following the dusty Dry Ridge Road for about two miles, you would arrive at our farm and our two-story, white house sitting slightly above the road on the left. My cousins lived about a quarter mile from us.

Mom would likely be in the garden picking beans, or in the backyard preparing to wash clothes. Every time she washed, she would examine our clothes and fuss over finding new holes and tears.

Dad might be struggling to piece together a harness and get it on one of the horses while getting ready to plow the tobacco, or, if it was a Sunday afternoon, he might be cutting a neighbor's hair in the shade of a tree. While we were living in Ohio, he had worked as a part-time barber, and after moving to Big Clifty, he often cut my uncles' and even our neighbors' hair for free.

Meanwhile, Billy and I would either be in the tobacco patch chopping weeds, drawing and heating water so Mom could do the washing, or in between those tasks, perhaps hanging out under one of the shade trees working on an old bicycle. Doug would likely be playing with a cat or sitting on the edge of the pond watching turtles crawl out of the water and onto rocks to soak up the sun. He also might be playing with the large white rabbit someone had given us. The rabbit had the run of the place and was not bothered by our dogs. Juanita was still very young and would most likely be playing house on the front porch with her rag doll and trying to get it to sit up straight so it could eat the mud pies she had made.

If you drove that same route today, you would notice that not much has changed except that all the small grocery stores and banks are long gone, and several more houses have been built along the roads. The gravel road has been paved over, is still narrow, and has no white or yellow line in the middle.

Houses

Both our East View and Big Clifty houses had galvanized metal roofs, making it easy for us to tell when it was raining by the loud noise of rain hitting the roof. There was no insulation between the roof and the living areas to block the sound. Each house also had front and back porches.

Our Eastview house had two stories, but the upstairs rooms were unheated because they didn't have access to a chimney for a stove. We also didn't really need the space, so we only used those rooms for play areas and storage.

Our Big Clifty house was originally a single-room, large log cabin that was built much earlier from hand-hewn logs. The log cabin served as our living room, and additional rooms for bedrooms and a kitchen had been added. Inside, sheet rock, along with old paper for insulation, had been applied over the logs. Outside, mud chinking had originally been placed between the logs, and later, wood siding had been installed over the logs and chinking. The chinking was beginning to break up, and cold air could enter the house through the siding and the thin paper insulation.

We had only the bare minimum of furniture in the house, and what we did have served a useful purpose. Our houses had only a couple of small built-in closets, so we usually had one or two large free-standing wardrobes for our clothes.

The wardrobes had drawers at the bottom for socks and underwear. However, we usually stored just about everything in those drawers along with our underwear. The drawers were just right for holding slingshots, interesting rocks, and anything else we wanted to keep, such as apples we planned to use in setting snares for rabbits.

Of course, most of the time, we would throw our clothes on the floor in a pile near the bed. It seemed useless to us to have to hang them up and then take them down first thing the next morning to wear them again.

Pots and pans were kept in the oven of the stove or hung on the walls.   A free-standing metal cabinet held most of the dishes and utensils. The cabinet had storage space, including a flour bin at the bottom and a hand-cranked flour sifter above the countertop.

Our Barn

The barn was the center of activity on our farms. Nearly everything we did, in some way, involved the barn. The farm animals used it for shelter and a place to eat, and we used it for milking, storing feed, including hay and corn fodder, and protecting a few tools and equipment from the weather. It also made a great playground, especially during rainy and cold weather. We could climb around on the rafters, play hide-n-seek, shoot at each other with our homemade pop guns, or just hang out in the barn, solving world problems or planning our next fishing trip.

Our barns always had a wide pull-through hallway in the center, with both ends open. Stalls were on both sides of the hallway for the animals. In addition, there were one or two sheds with gates at each end that could be left open or closed. Usually, the gates had been knocked loose by an agitated cow or horse and had to be propped up against one side of the shed and held in place at the other end with baling wire.

Baling wire was versatile and used back then much as duct tape is used today. Some people called it Farmer's

Welder because it could be twisted tight around just about anything. For instance, we used it to hold mufflers on cars, to keep tier poles in the barn from sliding around when standing on them, to patch woven wire fences, and to serve as a temporary clothes line.

A loft spanned the entire barn, except for maybe one of the sheds. The loft had an opening at one end of the barn for moving hay into and out of the loft - it is visible in the photo of Dad and me.

Also, notice that the car in the background of the photo had what was called a suicide rear door that opened from the front. If the door opened inadvertently while moving, either from a fault or more likely a kid, the wind would slam the door open, possibly dragging the person out that was near the door.

We usually fed the horses and cows outside the barn so they wouldn't waste so much of the feed. However, in bad weather, we could toss hay directly from the loft down into the stalls and sheds.

Tobacco sticks for hanging the tobacco were usually kept in the loft or piled along the wall in one of the sheds. Some small tools, such as posthole diggers and tobacco setters, would be in the barn hanging on the wall of one of the sheds.

Sometimes, a hen that didn't want to follow the rule of laying her eggs in the chicken house would have a nest in the loose hay of the loft. Oftentimes, we wouldn't notice the nest until the eggs had started to hatch.

Dad and Sunburned me at our East View Home with the Barn and Tobacco Patch in the Background

A simple well-worn ladder, usually with one or two broken rungs, was used to climb into the loft.

Tobacco tiers, for holding the tobacco until it dried and was ready for stripping, were placed high up in the loft near the roof, leaving room below for the hay. There were always a couple of tiers that were loose and needed to be nailed down to reduce the risk of someone falling when standing on them while hanging the tobacco. But most of the time, we would forget to do that, and wouldn't think about it until we were actually standing on them again in the fall.

Our barns were usually in poor shape and leaning a bit, as the animals would sometimes knock the support posts off their foundation rocks and into the dirt, causing them to rot from the bottom up.

We built a new barn at our Big Clifty home site because the old one was in such poor shape that Dad was afraid it was past time for it to fall. It did fall, not long after the new barn was completed.

Billy and my uncle Junior essentially built the barn by themselves after a neighbor helped lay out the dimensions and set the support posts. The new barn was built strong and is still in use today.

Corn Crib

A small storage building called a corn crib was located near the barn and used primarily to store the corn that we hand-picked each fall.

Our corn crib that looked much like a big wooden box, had an entrance door, an opening for pitching the corn into the crib, and a wooden floor. We always pitched the ears of corn directly onto the floor of the crib. Occasionally, animals such as raccoons and even foxes would steal some of the corn if the door was left open or a board on the side of the building was loose or missing. When in the corn crib, we had to watch out for snakes that sometimes came in looking for mice.

Mom and Juanita with Corn Crib in Background

We always kept a wide flat shovel, called a corn scoop, in the corn crib to scoop up corn. We would shovel the corn into a large bucket and feed it to the horses and hogs, as they could eat the kernels of corn directly off the cob. Cows, though, had a more difficult time eating whole ears of corn, so we usually fed them crushed corn. When we were out of crushed corn, we gave the cows small ears called "nubbins" that they could eat whole, including the cob.

Moths loved the corn, and sometimes the air would be full of them as we scooped the corn into the buckets.

The Well

Our well, located at the rear of the house, was hand-dug and about 25 feet deep. We had a hand-operated water pump, but we used a rope and bucket to draw water when the pump was not working, which was often. During hot, dry summers, we had to really conserve water as the well would nearly go dry.

About every two or three years, Dad would decide it was time to clean out the well. He would wait until summer, when the well would be essentially empty with very little water running into it. I never heard my brother Billy agree that it was time to clean the well, because it required someone, usually him, to be lowered into the well with a rope tied around their chest. I was always glad I was considered too young for that job.

A candle was first lowered into the well to be sure there was enough oxygen at the bottom. Dad would then lower Billy to the bottom along with a bucket and a small scoop. Mud, frogs, and whatever else was there were scooped into the bucket and pulled to the surface. Most of the time, the well would be clean after removing four or five buckets of waste material.

Billy was always glad when that chore was complete, and he could get out of there. He still recalls being somewhat alarmed when, looking up from the bottom of the well, he could only see a small patch of daylight at the very top and no one in sight. He worried that Dad might have a heart attack, and no one else was strong enough to pull him out of the well. I recently told him he shouldn't have worried, because if we had to, we would have carried water from the pond and kept pouring it into the well until we floated him out. That rescue plan didn't seem to alleviate his worry. I think I know how he felt because 25 feet is a long way down a hole that gets smaller close to the bottom. Our well is visible in the background of the picture of the four of us siblings.

Outhouse

Our outhouse was a small wooden structure located a couple of hundred feet away from the house. It seemed much farther away if you had diarrhea or needed to use the toilet on a cold winter night. Frequently, we didn't want to go before bed, thinking we could hold out until morning. About five minutes later, and just as we were getting warm, we would realize we needed to use the toilet, and soon. We would wait as long as possible, and then make a mad dash for it in the dark. It was too much trouble to find and light a lantern, so we just hoped there was enough moonlight to keep us from running into the fence or falling over a dog.

Old Sears Roebuck catalogs were left in the outhouse, serving as both reading material and toilet paper. That double use of the catalog worked well as long as the paper hadn't gotten wet from rain or snow blowing through the wide cracks in the outhouse walls. I don't think it even dawned on us to put a small lidded box in the outhouse to keep paper, including the catalog, dry.

We added a bathroom to our home about the time I entered college. It was the last step in a long journey toward having indoor plumbing. We first needed electricity to pump the water. After getting electricity, an above-ground water pump was installed, providing running water in the kitchen. Running water was a big help to Mom in canning and washing dishes, but that was about all the water the well could furnish. However, I was relieved that we no longer needed to make sure there was a bucket of water in the kitchen before nighttime.

We later drilled a much deeper well, giving us sufficient water for all our needs, including a bathroom, without fear that the well would be pumped dry. I am sure Billy was glad that the old hand-dug well was abandoned, and his days of being lowered to the bottom to clean it were over.

The Pond

Every farm had to have a pond to provide water for the livestock. A few farms may have had a creek running through them and providing year-round water, but that was highly unusual. In addition to providing water for livestock, our pond was the water source for jobs such as watering the plants when setting tobacco. The pond also provided us with recreation. We would search the banks for frogs, skip rocks across its surface, and during the summer, sometimes use it as a swimming hole. But, we didn't do much swimming in the pond, because we would sink up to our knees in the thick bottom mud. In some places, the mud was like quicksand and would nearly hold anyone wading in it.

The pond froze over during extremely cold weather, forcing us to use an axe to break up the ice so the animals could get at the water. We skated on the ice, but usually ended up falling hard and getting hurt or getting our feet wet from breaking through thin ice near the edge of the pond. I can still hear the very unique sound the ice made as it cracked beneath our feet. Those cracking sounds were a warning that we'd better get off the ice, and quick.

Several times, we tried stocking the pond with fish we caught from the creek, a mile or two from our home. We would sometimes catch a few small sunfish and try to get them home and into the pond alive.

We never thought far enough ahead to take a water container for the fish, so we just carried them tied to a string. We didn't even hurry home but were always distracted, stopping many times along the way. By the time we got home, the fish were long dead and usually dried up from the hot sun.

I am not sure how it happened, but someone had managed to put one small Crappie fish into the pond. It lived and continued to grow even though the pond stayed muddy from the livestock and hogs regularly using it. Several years later, my brother Doug tried his luck fishing in the pond and caught the Crappie. By that time, it was really large - weighing around two pounds, which was far bigger than any fish we were used to catching. I don't know if he kept and ate the fish or returned it to the pond.

During one severe drought, our pond dried up, and so every afternoon we would drive our cows and horses a little over a mile to the creek for water. Most of the time, we didn't ride the horses but walked behind the animals as we followed a small path through the woods.

Driving them to the water was never a problem because they were thirsty and anxious to get there. Sometimes, when we were getting close to the creek, they would take off running and get far ahead of us. However, getting them to go back home often turned into a problem. Most of the grass in our pasture had dried up, so the horses and cows would want to stop and graze along the way back. Most of the time, unless we were in a real hurry, we would let them eat some of the green grass along the pathway.

Our Yard

The yard around the house was always well-worn as a result of our spending a lot of time in it playing and working on bicycles, etc. The edges of the yard were less used and often overgrown, needing trimming. We had an old hand-pushed lawn mower - the type that did not have a motor. We seldom used it – we didn't need to. Most of the grass, at least close to the house, was worn down to bare dirt, and the mower couldn't get close enough to the weeds growing in the fence rows.

Our shade trees were in the front yard, and usually one of them had a rope swing tied to a large limb with an old tire used for the seat. At least once, Dad made some whitewash from lime and painted the bottom four or five feet of the trees white. I am not sure if that was to protect the trees from bugs or simply to improve the look of the yard.

A large tub for heating water for washing clothes, along with a clothes line, was in the backyard near the well. There were usually a lot of clothes awaiting washing, even though we wore the same clothes for days and changed out of our school clothes as soon as we got home from school.

8

Our One Room School

I was in the second grade at school, and the teacher had just announced lunch time. All students dashed for the shelves to grab their lunch and hurry up and eat it so they could have the rest of the lunch period to play. Younger students had to watch out or get trampled by the older seventh and eighth-grade students in their rush to grab their lunches and be first out the door.

After retrieving my lunch sack, I hurriedly opened it, anxious to see what I had. I have no idea why I was so anxious to open it since I knew it was going to be a biscuit with either a sausage or a fried egg inside it. I liked both, although the canned sausage contained a lot of cold grease, making it not quite as tasty as the egg.

I realized I could be having peanut butter on my biscuit if we had not gotten into it and eaten it all up almost as soon as Mom brought it home. But we enjoyed it while it lasted, and our cold biscuit for lunch was just fine.

Mom would fry several sausages at a time and then, since we didn't have a refrigerator, put them in small fruit jars for use later in making our school lunches. After tightening the lid, she would set them on a shelf upside down so the grease would run down and help seal the lid.

Occasionally, Mom would use the money she got from selling cream to buy a jar of peanut butter. She intended to use it for making our school lunches. She wanted to give us something other than egg and sausage biscuits. But that usually didn't work out as she planned. Billy and I, and sometimes Doug, would find the peanut butter and eat most or all of it at once.

We would try to get Juanita to eat a little of it so she would also be guilty and maybe not tell on us. I guess we didn't realize that the empty jar would be all the evidence against us that Mom would need.

I can still hear Mom fussing when she discovered the peanut butter was gone. She would say, "I'm never buying another jar of it, and you kids will just have to keep having egg and sausage biscuits for lunch instead of peanut butter."

But, she soon got over her disappointment and would try the same thing later when she again had a little extra money. But, that usually worked out the same way with her making the same resolve to never, ever, buy peanut butter again.

A few kids had lunch boxes, but most of us brought lunch in paper bags that we would take home for reuse. As soon as we arrived at school, we would place our lunch boxes or bags on shelves mounted to the school wall.

Burkhead School, located about two miles from our Eastview home, was a one-room elementary school for grades one through eight. Most years, the school had a total of about 20 to 25 students, with each grade level having from zero to four students. I began attending Burkhead during the first grade and continued until about halfway through the seventh grade.

All students, including us, walked to school in rain, cold, snow, or whatever the weather we had. I don't recall how the teacher got there, but probably drove or was driven there by someone. All teachers, at least while I attended, were women.

The schoolhouse sat on a small hill with both boys' and girls' outhouses about 100 feet from the school and highly visible from the schoolroom. There was no place to wash our hands after using the outhouse. Even if there was, I doubt anyone would have actually gone to the trouble.

A large coal-burning pot-bellied stove sat in the center of the room. The front wall was mostly blackboard. Each student had their own assigned desk, which was actually just a seat with a small table as a writing surface and to hold books while they were reading. While school was in session, students had to remain sitting at their desk and raise their hand and ask permission to get up to for instance, to sharpen their pencil, get a drink of water, or go outside to the outhouse.

The school had neither electricity, indoor plumbing, nor a water well. An old cistern was near the schoolhouse, but apparently had been abandoned long before I attended the school.

Our drinking water was drawn by hand from a nearby neighbor's well using a rope and had to be carried to the school in a bucket. The bucket of water sat on a small table against the wall, easily accessible to younger as well as older students. We all drank directly from a shared dipper, which was a practice that undoubtedly would be frowned upon today.

Billy started going to Burkhead while in the third grade and attended there through the eighth grade. He then transferred to Lynnvale High School in White Mills. For at least a couple of years and until we moved to Big Clifty, Doug and I would turn left out of our driveway and walk the two miles to Burkhead. Billy would turn right and walk about three miles to Highway 84 and catch the school bus to Lynnvale.

All regular school work was accomplished using pencil and paper. A well-used pencil sharpener was mounted on the wall.

If we needed to use ink instead of lead, we had to use a fountain pen dipped into a bottle of ink. Ballpoint pens were not perfected yet. Each desk had an ink well, which was simply a hole on top sized to hold a bottle of ink. I don't remember ever actually using ink, but maybe once or twice. It was just too risky for a bunch of kids to be using ink. Invariably, most of the ink wound up on our hands or clothing, and sometimes in the hair of the kid sitting in front of someone who was just messing around with the ink.

When it was time for a particular class and subject matter, such as third-grade math, the third-grade students went to the front of the room and sat on a long bench. The rest of the student body was expected to stay at their desks and study, read, or whatever they could do quietly and without talking. I don't remember how many subjects were taught per grade level, but it couldn't have been more than two or three, because with only three subjects per grade level, the teacher would have had to hold 24 classes a day to go through all eight grades. I only remember the English, math, and reading classes, with maybe a little geography thrown in. But usually, two or maybe three grades had no students, which simplified the teacher's job.

We had a lot of time on our hands while the teacher was focused on the other grades. However, we knew it was not good for the teacher to have to stop what she was doing and reprimand us for being too loud or misbehaving. Therefore, we did a lot of note-passing during those times and occasionally couldn't resist throwing a paper wad at someone or simply annoying the person sitting in front of us.

Every few days, the teacher would select someone to take the blackboard erasers outside and beat them against a rock to clean out the chalk dust. A few of us were never selected, and we thought the reason was that she gave the task to her pet students.

However, now thinking back on it, I believe it was because those students would most likely clean the erasers and then come right back inside. Some others, including me, probably would have taken advantage of the opportunity to stay outside as long as we could. Also, more than likely, we would have gotten distracted by something else and wound up dusting only about one-half of the erasers or leaving several of them outside.

Printing things such as test papers was strictly a tedious mechanical process that took a lot of the teacher's time. She had to first prepare originals, or stencils, by hand on special paper. She would then transfer the image of each page to a Jelly Graph, which was really just a slab of firm gelatin. Ink was applied to the gelatin impression, and then one copy at a time was made from the impression. Since there were only two or three students in each grade, she only needed a few copies of each sheet of paper, but also, since there were as many as eight grade levels, she had to prepare as many as eight sets of originals.

Sometimes, older students helped with printing handouts or announcements to be taken home, such as an upcoming pie supper event or a small maintenance job needing a volunteer.

Doug didn't want to start school and objected to having to walk there. We had to almost drag him there for his first day. The next morning, he was sleeping soundly when Mom woke him up to get ready for his second day of school. He told Mom he got through yesterday, and so didn't need to go back. He almost went into shock when Mom told him there was no such thing as getting through, and he would have to keep going to school for 12 more years.

Many people believe one-room schools were a poor learning experience for the students, but I don't think so. For instance, if you were in the fourth grade, you were listening and watching the lessons being repeated for the second and third grades, and then you were getting a good glimpse of what you were likely to be studying and learning in the fifth through the eighth grades. Students who were paying at least a little attention could develop a good foundation and readiness for moving up to the next grade level. Also, all day long, you were associating with students of different grade levels– not just those of your own age. You learned from the older students, probably including a lot that should not have been learned.

I have lots of memories - most are good, some not from attending the one-room school. I dreaded Valentine's Day and even Christmas, because I felt they were actually popularity contests. I was always afraid of being embarrassed by having received the fewest valentines or the smallest Christmas present. Valentines were handed out to friends - boys and girls - early in the morning of Valentine's Day.   Then, all day long, some kids were bragging about how many they got and asking questions such as how many I got and who gave them to me.

We drew names for Christmas presents at least a month before Christmas and were supposed to keep the names secret. That didn't work very well, because most of the time, everyone knew who you drew and who drew your name before you even got back to your seat. It was embarrassing to open your present in front of the whole school, and maybe have an obviously cheap present, such as a pack of old maid cards, which was almost free at the 5 & 10 cent stores.

Morning and afternoon recesses were always fun, with the entire school often playing together. The very young first and second graders had to grow up fast, as a lot of our games involved rough-housing and getting run over by the older students. Softball was a favorite, but usually recess was about over by the time we chose up sides and found the bat and ball.

One of the games we played, which usually involved everyone, was called Ante Over. That game had very simple rules. The students divided themselves into two teams, with one team on each side of the school building. A ball was then thrown over the roof, and if caught before hitting the ground, everyone on both teams had to switch sides of the building without being touched with the ball. As soon as the ball was caught, everyone took off running one direction or the other around the building toward the other side. If the person with the ball could tag someone on the other team, then that person had to switch teams. Throwing the ball and running went on until recess was over. There was a lot of tension and much yelling since you didn't want to be tagged but couldn't tell who had the ball. I don't think anyone ever figured out or cared which team won because all we were actually doing was swapping people from team to team and getting in a lot of running and chasing after each other.

Another game we often played was called Red Rover, for which the students also divided into two teams. Each team would get on opposite ends of the school yard and form a line by holding hands. One team would then yell Red Rover twice and call someone's name on the opposite team. The named person then ran as hard as they could and tried to break through the other line. The person doing the running always chose what they considered to be a weak spot and slammed into the line, trying to break through. Often, weak spots were thought to be first or second-grade girls, but not always, since an older boy might be holding her hand really tight. The weak spot person often ended up getting hurt and crying. I am not really sure what the purpose of that game was, other than to also get in a lot of running.

Sometimes, several students would decide to take on a project that would keep us busy for days. One such project was building a leaf house. We would spend several recesses and lunch periods digging a large rectangular hole about two feet deep into the ground and then cover it with a roof formed from poles, leaves, or whatever we could find. Leaves were piled inside to keep us off the ground. We would play inside the leaf house for maybe one or two recesses and then forget all about it and go on to some other endeavor.

Burkhead School - 1947

The school photograph from 1947 is with Ms. Blandford as the teacher. I am in the first row, second from right, and Billy is in the same row, fourth from right. This photo must have been taken soon after school started in the fall because all students, except one or two, are barefoot.

Most of the kids went to school barefoot from the time school started in early September until cooler weather arrived, normally around the middle of October. After going barefoot all summer, it was difficult for us to make the transition to shoes, especially since the weather was usually still very warm.

The school photo from 1950, with Ms. Aubrey as teacher, must have been taken later in the year, since all the kids now have their shoes on. My brother Doug is far left in the front row; I am the first boy from the right in the third row. I am standing in front of the door wearing overalls; Billy is in the back row, second from left.

A traveling photographer or sometimes a local studio would come by once a year and take pictures of the students as a group, along with the teacher. Before printing the pictures,

Burkhead School - 1950

parents were asked how many they would like to buy. Although cheap compared to today's prices, many families could not afford a picture each year and would share the cost and the picture with a close relative.

During the winter, older boys, including me, sometimes arrived at school early before the rest of the students arrived. We would keep adding wood to the stove until it got really hot. We would then hold the end of the long metal fire poker in the fire until it was red hot and see how fast we could use it to drill holes in the floor around the stove. It wouldn't take long for the extremely hot poker to burn its way through the wooden floor.

I am not sure how we avoided accidentally burning the school down because the floor was well-seasoned wood that was periodically oiled to keep down dust. We eventually had so many holes in the floor, it is a wonder the stove didn't fall through to the ground beneath the school. We finally stopped drilling the holes, probably under serious threat from the teacher.

One winter, sparks from the stove nearly caught the school roof on fire. There were a lot of dry leaves piled around the chimney on the roof, and they caught on fire. The teacher really panicked. I didn't understand at the time why she was so excited, but now I know that allowing the schoolhouse to burn down on her watch wouldn't look very well on her resume and possibly even get her fired.

She yelled at us older boys to run as fast as we could to the neighbor's house and get water to put out the fire. Of course, no boy in his right mind would get the water, as we saw the burning of the school as a perfect once-in-a-lifetime opportunity to get rid of school, maybe forever. We figured we should just let it burn as that was the best possible thing to happen that day. Also there was no way we wanted the reputation of having helped save a schoolhouse. We could imagine the possibilities, including almost unlimited fishing, if there were no school.

The teacher finally had to tell the girls to go and get the water and put out the fire. All of us older boys watched and laughed as the girls climbed on the roof and poured water on the burning leaves.

After the fire was out, the teacher was pretty annoyed with us and ended up giving the ringleaders, including me, a whipping. We really didn't mind the whipping as we considered it a badge of honor and knew it would earn us the respect of the younger boys. Actually, what it did was earn me another whipping from Dad when I got home.

I remember dreading the whipping from Dad because, more than likely, he was going to be really mad. But I was surprised that the whipping seemed much lighter than I had been expecting. I didn't think much more about it then, other than being glad it was over. I now believe that even though it was a serious matter, Dad was still young enough to relate to and understand how boys might view, and try to take advantage of the situation. But, he had to go through with the punishment to reinforce his admonishment not to behave like that again.

Every time we got in trouble and received punishment at school, the teacher would write a note to our parents explaining what we did and the punishment we had received. Although I always dreaded giving them the note, it never occurred to me to throw it away. I never gave the notes to Dad, but would always give them to Mom, hoping she would intercede with Dad on our behalf. Billy missed out on those particular whippings because he had started ninth grade back at Lynnvale School.

For a while after that, it may have been our imagination, but it seemed the teacher was holding a grudge against us ringleaders and looking for any opportunity to again adjust our behavior. A couple of months later, just before Christmas, I had a real chance to do damage control and improve my relationship with the teacher, but I blew it.

The school always put up a Christmas tree two or three weeks before Christmas, and one day, right after lunch, the teacher told a couple of us older boys to take the hatchet, go into the woods near the back of the schoolhouse, and get a decent-looking cedar tree. She was planning on having a few students decorate the tree before school let out for the day.

She didn't realize it, but sending the two of us off the school grounds, and in the middle of the day, was like telling two death row inmates to leave the prison and bring back some cookies.

The second we legally stepped off the school grounds, we felt free as birds and immediately began exploring the nearby woods looking for the very best Christmas tree the school had ever had. We figured that would surely get us back into the teacher's good graces.

We found and cut down a few candidate trees, but kept finding fault with each one. Some had twisted tops, and others had limbs missing, giving them an unbalanced look. Before we knew it, we were at least a mile from the school and still didn't have a tree. We finally realized it was getting late, and we'd better take the next tree we found and head back.

When we arrived back at the schoolhouse, the students had already gone home, and the teacher was still there, but a nervous wreck, thinking we must have gotten hurt or lost. She was ready to try rounding up a few neighbors to begin searching for us.

The good news was that she only gave us a mild scolding because she was so relieved we were ok. I believe she knew we didn't intentionally take so long – just too many interesting distractions kept getting in our way. The bad news was that the tree we brought back was the worst-looking one of any we had cut that afternoon. Also, dragging it through the woods for a good mile gave it a well-worn, beaten-down look.

The next day, there were "what is that thing?" looks on several faces, but after loading it with decorations, it looked fine, at least to me.

Most students who went to Burkhead essentially grew up together as they attended the same school from first through the eighth grade. Walking home was usually the highlight of the day since everyone who lived in the same direction started together. Many a plot was hatched, world problems solved, and friendships strengthened or ended during the walks home.

I sometimes still wonder how some kids might begin the walk home as good friends, and then be throwing rocks at each other after only a half-mile. However, usually within another half mile, whatever caused the rock-throwing was forgotten, and a swimming trip to a nearby creek had been added to their plans.

One girl in the school usually avoided playing games with us during recess and seemed somewhat uppity to most of us boys. I don't remember the circumstances, but one day my cousin Leroy was mad at her and threatened to throw her down an old dried-up well, or cistern located in front of the school. The top of the cistern had been concreted over for years, so there was no way he could do that. Her parents came to school a few days later and told the teacher their daughter was having nightmares over the threat, and they wanted the culprit punished.

My brother Billy and I had heard him make the threat, but we were completely innocent. However, we allowed ourselves to get caught up in the incident. Leroy was trying to devise a plan to reduce his punishment and convinced me and

Billy that if we let him say we had put him up to it, his punishment might be far less. We should have smelled a rat, but that seemed like a reasonable plan at the time. The way we saw it, we weren't actually saying we made the threat, and so there was no reason for us to be punished. Besides, Leroy would see us as heroes and owe us for helping him out.

The plan didn't work out exactly as we planned. Dad found out about the threat but couldn't decide how involved Billy and I were, so he sent a note to the teacher suggesting she whip all three of us just to be sure she got all the guilty parties. Unfortunately, the teacher thought that was a good idea and decided to send a clear message and whipped us in front of the whole school. Usually, everyone else would be told to go outside while whippings were going on. Billy and I then got another whipping at home, which made our punishment even worse than what Leroy received.

We suspected Leroy may have exaggerated our involvement more than our agreed-upon plan. We planned possible pay-back options and held a grudge against him for at least a full day - then everything was back to normal.

I don't remember, and often wonder, how the teacher got the switch she used to whip us. The nearest trees were at least 100 feet from the schoolhouse, and it seems I would remember having to wait while she found a suitable switch. Billy doesn't remember either. She may have kept one at all times as a threat to misbehaving kids, or she may have whipped us with a paddle, and we have forgotten that little detail.

Once a year, the school held a fundraiser known as a Pie Supper - as much a social event as a fundraiser. These events gave the whole community, parents and kids, an opportunity to come together and have a little fun while catching up on the latest local news.

The older schoolgirls and other local girls would cook and donate a pie to be auctioned. The girl who made the pie would remain behind a sheet in front of an oil lamp such that only her shadow was visible to the audience. Even though she wasn't fully visible, there was little doubt who the girl actually was. The guys would bid on the pie, and the winner would get to eat it while sitting with the girl.

The bidding was fiercest and highest when the pie belonged to a pretty girl, and two or more guys were bidding against each other, trying to keep anyone else from getting it. The auctioneer would recognize the rivalry and encourage the bidders to keep bidding. Pies that sold for the most money gave the girl bragging rights, but usually broke the successful bidder.

The students, including me, were not interested in buying pies. We generally just hung around talking, making noise, and probably disrupting the event.

I remember one pie supper in particular. One night, a friend, somewhat older and bigger than me, and I decided to take a shortcut to the schoolhouse by crossing a neighbor's field rather than following the road. Even though we could barely see in the dark, we began racing each other across the field. We knew the field well enough that nothing could possibly go wrong.

Luckily for me, he was ahead of me about 15 feet when I heard a strange, loud crashing noise and him yelling. I was able to stop just before I saw him shoot past me, going backwards and still yelling. There was enough light for me to find him behind me, lying on the ground, but I still didn't know what had happened, and apparently, neither did he.

What we didn't know at the time was that the neighbor had just recently put up a new tall fence made of woven wire with strands of barbed wire on top. My friend had hit the fence at full speed in the dark, and the fence gave just enough to act like a slingshot and shoot him backwards about 10 feet.

He suffered only a sprained ankle and minor cuts, but both his shirt and pants were torn in several places. The fence was damaged a little, including a stretched barbed wire and one or two leaning posts.

We decided to give up the pie supper idea, and he limped back home. For some reason, he never did talk much about that experience, and we never told the neighbor about the fence. I guess the neighbor figured one of his cows must have tried to get out and had damaged it.

We always looked forward to the last day of school and had a lot of fun with a simple jingle, "School's out, School's out, the teacher wore her bloomers out." We would keep singing that until we were at least halfway home.

After I finished sixth grade, Burkhead School closed, and I started seventh grade back in Lynnvale School.

Decades after leaving Burkhead School, I had recurring dreams about being back there. We would be playing, and I would be terribly thirsty, essentially dying for a drink of water. But I was having too much fun playing and wouldn't take a drink because I knew it was a dream, and I would wake up if I so much as touched the water bucket. Eventually, I would get so thirsty I would have to stop playing and take a drink. Sure enough, as soon as I did, I would immediately wake up very thirsty. I am not sure how to interpret that dream other than one of those rocks we used to throw at each other may have hit me in the head.

Another recurring dream I used to have quite often was that I was back in Burkhead School, sitting at my desk, and suddenly realizing I was barefoot. I don't know why that was embarrassing in my dream, because everyone did go to school barefoot as long as possible before cold weather set in. Bare feet are visible in the 1947 school photo.

I occasionally drive by my East View home and on to the Burkhead School site. A residential home now sits where the school used to be. Workers must have done a lot of grading when building the home, as the bank that we jumped off of as kids, between the school yard and the road, is not nearly as high as I remember it. Also, the bridge over the small creek that crosses the road not far from the school site is now only about four or five feet high. I distinctly remember it being at least ten feet high. We used to dare each other to jump off of it, or, often just to save time, we would simply push each other off the bridge. Thankfully, no one was ever hurt jumping that far.

Surely the creek must now be partially filled in, or the bridge has been somehow lowered.

Another thing I don't understand, is how the road between my home and the school has become shorter than when we walked it as kids. Last time I was through there, I rechecked to see if the road may have been rerouted, but it doesn't appear so.

9

Coal Oil Lamps and Lanterns

One time while we were living in White Mills, Dad was lighting one of our coal oil lamps. He had accidentally tilted it too far to one side and didn't notice that some of the kerosene spilled out and onto the outside of the lamp.

When he struck the match and tried to light the lamp, the whole thing burst into flames. The flames started burning his hands because he was still holding the lamp. The door to the outside yard was open, so he gave the lamp a quick softball-style underhand throw through the door and out into the yard. Since the lamp was on fire, it was almost like throwing a Molotov cocktail at the chickens that were casually scratching for bugs in the yard. They quickly scattered.

I don't know what would have happened if the door had not been open or if he had missed and hit the wall. The lamp was full of kerosene, so we would most likely have been looking for another place to live.

Before our house in Eastview was wired for electricity, we used coal oil, actually kerosene, lamps for lighting inside our home and lanterns outside as portable lighting for working, hunting, and any other time we needed light. We may have had a few candles for emergency lighting, but I don't remember ever seeing them burning.

Lamps were actually quite simple with just three parts – a small glass tank for the coal oil, a metal burner mechanism for holding and adjusting the cloth wick, and a clear glass globe sitting on the metal burner and over the wick.

One of the Coal Oil Lamps I Used as a Child

Back then, if you drove by someone's house at night, it was hard to tell whether they were still up or already in bed. Even if they were still up, the house would be dark except for a faint glow from their oil lamp, usually visible in only one window. Today, most houses are lit up at night, not too different from an airport runway.

The lamps were dangerous and could actually burn the house down if not used correctly. The air coming out of the top of the lamp globe was so hot that one could light a cigarette by holding it over the lamp. I never used that method to light anything, and now it seems it might be a good way to wind up without eyebrows or hair.

Most of the time, we had one lamp lit at a time to conserve coal oil, and that one lamp might be in the living room. But, if Mom happened to be cleaning up from supper or finishing up canning for the day, another would be in the kitchen.

When someone needed, for instance, to temporarily go into another room at night, they would likely take the one in the living room with them, leaving everyone else in the dark until they returned with the lamp.

Billy and I both remember that we would often be working on a puzzle or putting together a gadget at a small desk while using one of the lamps. Mom would need to go to one of the bedrooms to get her shoes, sweater, or something else, and would pick up our oil lamp as she went by us.

All of sudden, we would be sitting in the dark and have to wait until she came back with the lamp. We would then get back to whatever we were doing until the next time someone needed to use our lamp.

Since we had no TV, and it was somewhat difficult to read by oil lamps, we played a lot of checkers and sometimes listened to a battery-powered radio. We made paper airplanes and other small toys from whatever we could find.

We often stayed outside until nearly bedtime during the summer, so lamps were not used as much. I would often lie in the yard after dark, watching lightning bugs or hoping to see a falling star.

We would have to use lanterns for light when we were outside at night finishing our work such as milking, or stripping the tobacco. Lanterns were much like coal oil lamps, but ruggedly designed to be carried outside, even in rainy or windy conditions. They were made of metal, except for a glass globe, and had a handle for convenient carrying.

Lanterns were also dangerous, especially when using them in the barn and around extremely dry hay. Many a barn fire was started by an animal knocking over a lantern. It is widely believed that a cow kicked over a lantern, starting the Chicago fire of 1871.

A Coal Oil Lantern I Used as a Youngster

10

Caring for Our Livestock

One morning in late January, I awoke to a snowfall of six to eight inches. It was still snowing, but not as hard as when I had gone to bed. Dad had built a fire, but the heat had not reached into the back bedroom where Doug and I were covered so deeply in quilts we could barely move.

I didn't want to get up, but I knew that by the time Billy and I fed the livestock, milked, and got ready, it would be time to head for school. It would take a little longer to feed and walk to school because of the deep snow.

Mom wondered if we even needed to go to school, as the teacher and other kids might not show up. But there was no way of knowing for sure unless we went ourselves.

Most of the time, feeding the animals was not very difficult, but I always dreaded feeding during heavy snows and especially when it was really cold. Our heavy overshoes (we called them Arlecs) and gloves, if we could find them, made it hard to climb into the barn loft and use the pitchfork to throw hay down to the cows and horses.

For some reason, most farm people always called feeding the animals "doing up the work."

We didn't have many horses or cows because we kept only those few farm animals that we needed to work the farm or were otherwise useful in providing food or income for the family. On small farms, such as ours, we had to be really careful not to have more animals than the number of acres and our farm land could support. Dad had to choose, for instance, between keeping another horse to help with the farm work or another cow to ensure enough milk for the family.

Each animal we kept meant additional acres would be needed for pasture, and for growing more corn and hay to ensure adequate year-round feed. It also meant we had more work to do in harvesting the hay and in feeding the animals during winter. Keeping too many animals would also make it harder to get through winter without having to buy expensive feed.

During the summer, our horses and cows grazed in the pasture and didn't need to be fed. However, during the winters, they had to be fed hay at least once per day. Several times we had to ration feed during winters that were harsher or longer than usual. During those times, we usually cut back from three pitchforks of hay for each horse to just two.

The horses and cows usually ate together, so we would climb into the barn loft and throw down enough hay to last all of them all day. If our hay supply began to run short and we had to reduce the amount we fed each day, the horses would try chasing the cows away. If they kept doing that, then we would have to drag hay for the cows to a different location away from the horses.

The hogs were fed twice a day since they would immediately eat everything we gave them, or else waste it by spilling it and trampling it into the mud. It almost seemed to me they intentionally destroyed what they couldn't eat right away.

I always hated feeding the hogs because they would fight for position at the trough, making it hard to pour food for them without spilling half of it on myself. The feed trough needed to stay close to the fence, so you wouldn't have to enter the hog lot carrying food. The hogs could easily knock you down and hurt you while trying to get the food.

The chickens could essentially take care of themselves during the summer, but we still fed them some corn so they would remain close to the chicken house and not go completely wild. We shelled the corn using a hand-operated corn Sheller mounted on the side of a wooden box. The shelled corn would fall directly into the box, making it easy to scoop it out with our hands and put it into our feed bucket. We had to increase their feed during the winter as there weren't enough bugs, seeds, and other things for them to scratch up and eat.

We kept one or two sows for raising litters of pigs. A good sow could give birth twice a year, to litters of about eight piglets. Unfortunately, it wasn't uncommon for one or two in each litter to not survive—either crushed accidentally by the sow or killed by the boar hog.

Although hogs were a valuable cash crop and provided our meat, they required lots of care. They were natural rooters, constantly digging under fences and barn stalls. Dad put rings in their noses to keep them from digging holes under the fence and escaping their enclosures. This helped, but it didn't completely stop them, especially after a rain when the ground was softer than usual.

Pigs would squeal continuously while being held to install the nose rings, and I can't say I blame them—I'd squeal too if someone were punching holes in my nose without any pain reliever.

All male pigs and calves were castrated while still small enough to be held down. My granddad was our go-to person to perform the surgery, while the rest of us would help catch and hold the next victim. He could use his super-sharp pocket knife to complete the operation really fast, as long as we could keep the animal perfectly still. When through, he would splash alcohol on the wound, and the pig or calf would jump up and, in no time, be eating and acting as if nothing had happened.

There was so much squealing and bawling from the ones being worked on, I would wonder why the other males didn't run far away. But they just seemed curious about what was going on, and hung around the barn until we came for them. They did seem a little harder to catch than usual, so they must have finally realized what was happening and decided they wanted no part of it.

Most cattle in the 1940s grew horns. We always removed those when they grew big enough to hurt other cattle or us. I never wanted to help or watch while our cows were being de-horned, as it seemed to really hurt them, and sometimes it was bloody.

The cow's head, being dehorned, was tied tightly against the barn wall so she could hardly move. Then a large, long-handled tool that looked and worked much like a bolt cutter was placed over the horn with the cutting blades positioned close to the skull. The horn was severed as the handles were closed. Usually, and for a few minutes, a small stream of blood would spew out of the cow's head where the horn had been. The other horn was then removed in the same manner.

I can still hear the crushing sound as the blade cuts through a cow's horn. Back then, it was just part of the work. Today, most cattle are bred without horns, sparing both farmer and animal that harsh chore.

Dad said he would do the milking and feeding since he couldn't do any other work that day because of the snow. That was good news to Billy and me, so we hung around the house for a while, then Billy headed off for school, and I followed him a few minutes later. He needed to get there before everyone else because the teacher was paying him ten cents a day to arrive a little early and build the fire in the big pot-belly stove sitting in the center of the schoolhouse floor. Since the teacher probably wouldn't show up, he doubted he would get paid for building today's fire.

It was difficult walking to school that morning because there had been no traffic on the road to forge a path. We were still wearing our Arlecs over our shoes, and the extra weight began to tire us out by the time we got there. We walked through the deep snow by lifting our feet high as in marching.

Billy started the fire, and we waited in the schoolhouse for about an hour, but only a couple of other kids who lived close by showed up. Even the teacher didn't make it. I remember thinking that school wasn't so bad that day, without a teacher. It was almost fun being in the schoolhouse by ourselves. We all messed around for a while, but after getting good and warm by the hot stove, we all headed back through the snow for home.

Billy was excited that the teacher paid him the ten cents for building the fire, even though it wasn't needed that day.

Faithful Dogs & Wild Cats

We always had one, and sometimes two, dogs and a couple of cats. The dogs hung around the house and were good companions. They alerted us when unwanted visitors such as groundhogs, snakes, and skunks showed up. They also helped in rounding up livestock that had gotten out of the fenced areas and, once in a while, treed a squirrel, allowing us to shoot it and have it for supper. Mostly, though, they followed us everywhere we went, not wanting to miss out on anything we might get into or do.

We never allowed our dogs or cats into the house. Occasionally, one would find the door slightly open and walk in. Mom would grab the broom, and it wasn't long before the trespassing dog or cat found themselves being swept back out the door.

We often got the blame for things the dogs actually started, making them just as guilty, or guiltier, than we were. We sometimes got hurt trying to rescue them from places they shouldn't have been. Also, they would occasionally find a skunk and keep aggravating it until all of us got sprayed.

The worst thing they would do was get into a fight with another dog and cause us to get bitten trying to separate them. One of our dogs and one of my uncle's dogs couldn't stand each other and would fight nearly every time they were with my cousin and me. Their posturing and snarling at each other would go on almost continuously, and often would wind up in a physical fight if either one of them was a little more aggressive than usual.

One day, we were going swimming and had stopped to investigate a hole in a tree that just happened to be near a neighbor's electric fence wire. Our dogs were, as usual, circling each other, seemingly daring the other to start something. My dog inadvertently walked under the electric fence, and his raised tail came into contact with the live wire. He must have thought the other dog had bitten him, as he immediately spun around and ferociously leaped on my cousin's dog and grabbed him by the throat.

It was obvious he wanted to hurt or kill the other dog, making it almost impossible to separate them. We finally broke up the fight, but not before my cousin's dog had an ear partly torn off and barely escaped being choked to death.

My cousin's dog probably wondered what happened to cause my dog to attack him so viciously.

For some unknown reason, a few dogs develop a liking for raw eggs and gain a reputation as an "egg-sucker". If anyone was inquiring about a dog, the first question they would ask was, "Is he an egg-sucker?" Answering "yes" meant you were likely to remain the dog's owner because the person wanting a dog would have nothing to do with that one. Given the opportunity, egg-suckers can eat a lot of eggs.

While growing up, I never heard of anyone buying a dog. You could always find someone willing to give them away or maybe trade two for one.

I never understood why we called it "sucking" eggs, since every dog I saw doing that just broke the shell and lapped up the contents. I suspect they develop the habit by finding a hen's nest in a fence row, or somewhere else it shouldn't be, and giving it a try.

At least once, we had a dog with the habit of sucking eggs. He would actually go into the chicken house and take an egg out of a nest. That aggravated Mom a lot. He was an excellent guard dog and was much like a family member; otherwise, he would have been quickly banned from our farm.

She tried to break him of the habit by slipping doctored eggs into the hen's nest. She would make a small hole in one end of the egg and pour in red pepper, hoping it would break him of the habit. She also boiled an egg and tried to get him to eat it while it was steaming hot. However, nothing worked.

For all I know, he may have become addicted to eggs, or maybe he developed a taste for red pepper in his raw eggs.

The dog lived to a ripe old age, still sucking every egg he could find. We reduced his opportunities to get to the eggs by repairing the chicken house and trying to beat him to any nests the chickens made elsewhere.

Most of the time, our cats were much shorter-term residents than the dogs. We would just be getting used to having two or three particular cats around the place, and a little later, most of those would be gone, and new cats would show up. Some showed up because rural people back then had a habit of dropping off extra cats near other people's houses and barns.

The cats had only one job - keep down the mouse population in the barn and corn crib. They essentially fended for themselves with an occasional morsel or a little milk from us. We would play with them by dragging a cotton ball or a small stick on a string and watching them pounce on it.

I have no idea why I have a cat on my head in the photo. Both the cat and I look very uncomfortable.

Every once in a while, we would have a stray cat that was wilder than most and wouldn't let us touch it. Sometimes, it would seem friendly enough, and we would try to pick it up and pet it. However, most of the time, we wound up with major scratches and sometimes a bite or two. Every time we were bit bad enough to have to tell Mom and get treatment, she would warn us to stay away from that cat, and if she could catch it, she would wring its neck.

The Hay Field

Soon after the first frost, about the middle of October, our pastures would die back and not be able to provide sufficient grass for the livestock. This situation usually lasted through the winter and into the middle of May when pastures began to green up again.

During that time, we had to feed our horses and cows hay, and before winter set in, make sure we had enough stored to last through all those winter months.

About the middle of June, we would fence the horses and cows off of one of our fields and let the grass grow so we could cut it for hay. Just before frost, we would cut the hay with a heavy sickle mower – we called it a mowing machine – requiring two horses to pull it.

The sickle mowers were really dangerous as they had a 6-foot blade with around 30 double-edged, extremely sharp cutting knives. We needed to be very careful in keeping our fingers away from the cutting knives, especially when raising or lowering the cutting bar. The blade would sometimes move a small amount, but enough to sever a finger if not careful.

After the hay had dried for a day or two, Billy or Dad would use our horse-drawn hay rake and rake it into long rows. The raking job was fairly easy, except for the dust and shaking created by the tines lifting and falling back down. One horse could easily pull the light hay rake.

The rake operator sat on a seat in front of the rake, just behind the horse's heels, making it a dangerous job. If the operator accidentally fell off the rake, he would almost certainly fall in front of the rake directly behind the horse's rear feet. Also, if the horse became spooked and bolted, the rider could not jump off without risking falling in front of the rake. But luckily, neither Billy nor Dad ever had a serious accident while using the mower or the rake.

I tried using the rake at least once, mostly to see if I could. But the foot levers were too tight and far away for me to operate them reliably. The windrow I made looked like a snake crawling across the field rather than a straight line.

After the hay was raked, one of us would drive the horses and wagon along the windrows, while one or two others would use pitchforks to pick up and load the hay on the wagon. We then hauled the hay to the barn and again used pitchforks to pitch the hay from the wagon into the barn loft. Someone in the barn loft would drag the hay to the rear of the loft and pile it for use later in feeding the livestock.

Storing the hay in the loft was probably the worst part of harvesting hay. The entrance to the barn loft was well above our heads, even when standing on the wagon bed. The hay had to be tossed almost straight up to get it into the barn loft.

Inevitably, much of the hay would fall back on the head and back of the person tossing it up from the wagon bed. That was not a fun job, especially when you were in the hot sun and sweat bees were driving you crazy. The sweat bees, along with itching caused by hay falling down your neck, would make you yearn for a quick swim in the cold water of the creek. Actually, you would gladly jump into any water - even the pond at the back of the barn that was full of turtles, mud, and cows up to their bellies trying to stay cool.

Me with a Cat on My Head

Our Old Horse-drawn Hay Rake with Missing Shafts

During the winter, it was a daily chore to use the same pitchforks and throw the hay back down from the barn loft to feed the livestock.

Dad figured there must be a better way to store and feed the hay to the horses and cows. He decided it might be much easier to pile the hay into a stack and let them help themselves. That sounded like a good idea to Billy and me since we wouldn't have to climb into the barn loft every morning and throw down hay.

We started the stacks by setting two poles in the ground, much like fence posts, but at least 15 or 20 feet tall. We then, as usual, picked up the hay from the raked windrows in the field using pitchforks, but instead of storing it in the barn loft, we stacked it around the poles.

Just as Dad planned, the cows and horses helped themselves to the hay. But after a month or two, Dad became worried because the livestock were obviously wasting much of the hay by pulling it out of the stacks and trampling on it. Also, since they didn't have much else to do, they tended to hang out around the stacks and snack on the hay all day long. At the rate they were using it, there would not be enough hay to last the winter.

We finally had to build a fence around the stacks to keep the animals away. Then each day we had to climb to the top of the stack and pitch hay down to the ground.

Feeding from the stacks was actually much harder on us than from the barn loft. The stacks were outside in the cold and wind, and snow and ice accumulated on the stacks, making it difficult to remove the hay. The next year, no one mentioned stacking the hay in the field again, and so we reverted to our original method of storing it loose in the barn loft.

While I was still a young teenager, my grandfather had an old hay baler that made square bales - the bales were actually rectangular but were referred to as square, and they used wire to tie the bales rather than string. Two people had to ride at the very back of the baler to tie the wire each time the baler pushed a bale through the chute.

One day while watching them bale hay, I decided it would be neat to ride the baler and feed the wires.

I convinced my granddad to let me give it a try. I remember him grinning and saying, "Ok, but you might want to put on a shirt". I had come over to his house barefoot and without a shirt, but didn't really see why I would need one since all I would be doing was riding on the baler and poking wires through the bales.

As soon as the baler began to move, I knew I had made a mistake, but was not about to admit it. The baler was noisy, and the shaking was almost throwing me out of my seat. In addition, as it pounded the hay into bales, I was continuously in the middle of a dust storm that could easily be seen from miles away. Before we had made the first bale, I was covered with hay and dust, and sweat bees were trying to eat me alive, especially on my sweaty, bare back.

Thankfully, after one round through the field, my granddad said I had done a good job, but the other guy was rested and ready to take back over. I looked and felt like a walking zombie. I had both hay and dust in my hair, in my eyes, and everywhere else, but I tried to act disappointed that I was being pulled off the baler. I am sure no one believed that, but I didn't care – I just wanted to get away from that terrible baler.

I am now glad I did ride the baler, even for that short time period, as it was an experience I will never forget.

11

Visiting Grandparents in the Mountains

We knew our paternal grandparents as Mam & Pap. We would usually visit them in the Appalachian Mountains near Salyersville, Kentucky, about twice a year. The most memorable visits were in autumn during apple season. A tall apple tree grew within a few feet of the house, so close that at least half of its limbs reached over and high above the roof. It seemed the tree was trying to protect the house from alien invaders.

At night, just as I'd be drifting off to sleep, an apple would fall, smack the metal roof like dropping a cannonball on it, and then bounce and roll for what felt like an entire minute. Sometimes, two or more would fall in rapid succession, almost like a chain reaction. I half expected one to punch straight through the roof and hit me on the head. The worst part was trying to guess when the next one would fall so it wouldn't be such a surprise. A double-barreled 12-gauge shotgun, with both barrels firing inside the bedroom at the same time, would have made less noise.

I slept about as well as anyone would have if trying to sleep in the middle of an active artillery range.

Neither Mam nor Pap heard a thing, of course —years of apples bombarding the roof had deafened them to the racket. The next morning, after my sleepless night, Mam asked, "Did any of those apples fall and wake you up?" I could barely see her through my half-shut, sleepy eyes, but would answer "No, they must have all fallen off before we went to bed".

Dad seldom decided ahead of time when we would go visit, or if he did, he didn't mention it until the last possible moment. It was always spur of the moment to the rest of us, including Mom.

I think his decision to make the trip was after he had reached a milestone with the crops, such as having just finished hoeing the tobacco or plowing the corn and "laying it by". He probably could see a short break of a couple of days before beginning the next major farm effort, such as cutting hay or harvesting potatoes. Usually, it was right after supper, and nearly dark, when he would start looking for his hat and say, "Get ready, we are going to the mountains." He always wore a hat when going farther than a few miles from home. I don't remember what getting ready was all about because mostly all we had to do was climb in the car. Maybe that was his way of saying we'd better use the outhouse. We never took a suitcase or a change of clothes as we would only be there a couple of days.

Mom would throw together some jelly sandwiches, fill a gallon jug with water, and put those and a blanket or two in the car so we could have a snack to eat and covers to stay warm during the long ride.

Dad would check the tires, top off the coolant in the radiator, and place a gas can in the trunk just in case we ran out of gas before reaching the next gas station. He would also make sure we had materials and tools for patching and repairing flats we might have along the way.

He didn't have to check the spare tire because we didn't have one. It was very unusual for anyone I knew to have a spare tire. If they did have a spare at one time, it long ago replaced one of the other four that had suffered a blowout or had become irreparable for some reason. I actually remember the first spare tire I ever saw. It seemed strange to me that anyone would be carrying a perfectly good tire around in their trunk rather than having it on one of the wheels.

The first stop on our trip was at a relative's or a neighbor's house to see if they could check on the livestock and milk the cows while we were gone.

Our trips were before the advent of interstates and city bypasses, so we had to follow major highways through cities, including Elizabethtown, Bardstown, Lexington, and Mount Sterling. I did everything I could to stay awake and see all the sights, especially as we passed through the towns. However, most of the time, all of us except Dad were sound asleep and didn't even wake up for a short stop to get gas. That very well may be the reason we always went at night. He knew everyone would go to sleep and they wouldn't be picking on each other or asking a bunch of questions, such as, "How much longer?"

Dad worried a lot about the car being able to make it up the steep, winding hill near West Liberty, KY, without overheating. More than once, we had to stop and wait beside the road while the motor cooled enough to remove the radiator cap and refill it using our leftover drinking water. Once over that hill, he relaxed, and we pretty much had it made into Salyersville.

If we left home just before dark, then it would be two or three in the morning by the time we arrived at Mam and Pap's house. We would always show up as a complete surprise to everyone, as no one had a phone in those days. The only warning they had was possibly a letter written months earlier saying we might come up soon.

Mam and Pap - My Paternal Grandparents

Once, when we arrived near one AM, Mam told us to go wake up Dud, her brother, who sometimes stayed with them, and take his bed. She said he wouldn't care because it was almost time for him to get up, and besides, he had slept long enough anyway.

I wondered how he could have slept long enough by one o'clock in the morning. I also wondered why he didn't protest at all when we shook him awake and told him we needed his bed. He just said "ok" and got up. After greeting the rest of our family, he drank a cup of coffee and left the house for work.

I found out later that he always got up at one or two in the morning and left the house for "work." I am not sure, but his "work" might have had something to do with moonshine.

Mam and Pap were first cousins - their fathers were brothers. Actually, it wasn't really that unusual for cousins to marry at that time, especially in the mountainous areas. Many area roads were mostly dirt, making travel and meeting others much more difficult than today.

Marriage between cousins looks different on a genealogy tree. Since my grandparents were first cousins, they both had the same paternal grandparents.

Pap was 75 when he died, and Mam lived to be 98. She was hoping to make it to 100 because she grew up living with her grandmother, who had lived to 100 - she wanted to do the same. She almost made it.

When going up the lane to Mam and Pap's house, a seam of coal was clearly visible on the side of the hill near a small creek. When needing coal, all anyone had to do was use a pickaxe and dig it out.

Mam and Pap's house was surrounded on three sides by tall hills. After they got a TV, the antenna had to be mounted at the very top of one of the hills in order to receive signals from the TV stations. Cabling, nearly a quarter mile long was required to route the signal to the TV.

The distance from the TV to the antenna made it difficult to align the antenna with the desired TV stations. Without phones or radios, using smoke signals between the house and the top of the hill might have made the antenna alignment task

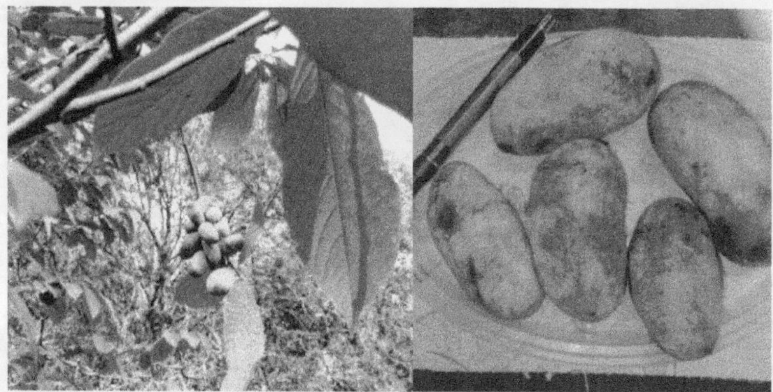

Pawpaws: On Tree (Left) and Ripe (Right)

easier.

A hand-dug well was located in the backyard and a small fish was usually kept in it to eat the bugs. I never asked how the practice of using the fish got started. I am sure it was clean, healthy water, but it always seemed to me as if it tasted a little like fish.

When we were visiting in the early fall, I would hear my relatives talk about going Pawpaw hunting. I had never seen a Pawpaw and, at the time, didn't really know what they were. Pawpaw trees are relatively small and fairly widespread in the Eastern Kentucky Mountains. They produce a fruit that looks, tastes, and smells much like a short banana.

They don't last long after ripening, as people and small animals, including squirrels, compete to be first to get to the ripe Pawpaws.

After spending a couple of nights at my grandparents, we would load up apples and a few garden items they were sending back with us, and then head home.

Dad with his Mom and Siblings - From Left: Ace, Nola, Robert, Mary Lola, Lonnie (Dad), Chloe (Dad's Mom), Dago - Not Shown Fred and Lacy

Our Big Clifty farm adjoined the farm of my other grand-parents (Mom's parents), who lived a little over a half mile away. They also used wood for heat, but burned it in a fireplace rather than in a stove, as we did. The fireplace did a reasonably good job of heating the room it was in, but other rooms usually stayed pretty cool.

I always liked to go visit them, especially during cold weather, when we would sit or hang around the fireplace. Every once in a while, I would have to rotate my body so the front could cool off at the same time my back was heating up. I would be the only child there, and I remember how quiet it got when no one was talking. The ticking of the wind-up clock on the mantle would be the noisiest thing in the room and sounded as if someone was tapping on the side of a dishpan.

Sometimes, one of my uncles would be lying on the couch, taking a nap. I always thought it strange that anyone would purposely want to sleep during the daytime. As kids, the days were not long enough to waste time sleeping. There were always trees to climb, toys to make, and if time permitted, going swimming or simply hanging around the yard playing with the dog.

12

Burley Tobacco Was Our Lifeline

I don't remember why, but it seems Dad always burned tobacco beds at night, usually taking all night and into the next day. This was about the only fun part of growing tobacco, as we enjoyed hanging around the huge fire and throwing on additional brush. I especially liked pitching large limbs with lots of dead leaves onto the hot coals. As soon as I did that, there would be a loud sizzling noise, like bacon frying in a skillet, and flames would immediately shoot upward, and sparks would fly as high as the nearby trees. A few went even higher, as if trying to reach the stars shining brightly overhead.

During one cold January night, a brother of Dad's was visiting from the mountains and helping him burn the tobacco bed. I couldn't stay up all night to help because it was a school night. But before going to bed, I decided to walk over to the woods and watch the burning for just a little while. When I got there, Dad's brother was lying beside the burning bed with his head resting on our dog as a pillow. I will never forget him saying, "You look tired, drag up a dog and lie down".

Burley tobacco is mostly grown in Kentucky and Tennessee and is primarily used in making cigarettes. This type of tobacco grows especially well in central Kentucky and was the primary cash crop for many small farms, including ours. It was grown solely to sell, as we used none of it ourselves.

Nearly every farm in central Kentucky grew Burley tobacco. For many families, the annual tobacco crop meant having money for necessities like shoes, winter coats, or school supplies. It was often the only dependable cash crop, and so important that everyone planned all their activities around raising tobacco.

Even our school schedules were set to allow kids to be home during critical times of need in the tobacco patch. The school year was set to end in the latter part of May, in time for kids to help set the tobacco plants, and didn't begin again until after Labor Day, when most tobacco would have been cut and housed in the barn.

Money from the sale of the tobacco was used to pay property taxes and pay off accumulated debt at the grocery and other stores.

Raising burley tobacco was essentially a year-round, labor-intensive job. From early spring through the fall, families—parents and kids—worked side by side in the fields and barns, doing the hard work, such as setting out the tobacco, and the lighter work, such as topping it. Neighbors helped one another set plants and house the crop, often sharing tools, wagons, and labor in a kind of rural barter system.

If you needed help from a neighbor, you kept up with the number of days the neighbor helped you, and when he needed help, you would pay him back by working at least the same number of days for him. Quite often, I would hear someone say something like "I owe him three days of work".

We began preparing the seedbed for the tobacco plants in late January or early February by cutting and piling brush and small logs to be burned. The bed was burned to kill weed seeds and hopefully most of the insects that had tunneled underground. The ashes also provided nutrients for the young plants. A tobacco bed about eight feet wide and 80 feet long would usually supply enough plants for one acre of tobacco.

Tobacco seeds were so small that only a spoonful was enough for the entire tobacco bed.

During May, after the threat of frost, the tobacco plants were pulled from the bed and set out in rows in the tobacco patch. Most of the time, we waited until it rained to set them out. It was easier, and the wet ground prevented the young plants from dying.

We used a string as a guide to make sure the tobacco plants were set out in a fairly straight row. The row needed to be reasonably straight, not only to look good, but to help when plowing the tobacco.

One person would drop the plants about a foot apart, and a second person would bend over and set them out by first gouging a small hole in the ground with a stick, or if it was really wet, by simply using the fingers.

After finishing a row, the string was moved over about four feet to mark the next row.

I can still almost feel the wet mud squeezing between my bare toes as I punched holes in the ground and inserted the plants.

The constant bending over to set out the plants was back-breaking for adults, but kids had no problem with it. We often completed an entire row of two or three hundred feet before standing up straight.

If the plants were ready to be set out, but the ground was too dry, we used a hand-operated tobacco setter that held water in a small tank. One person would jab the setter into the ground, and a second person would toss a tobacco plant, root first, into the setter. The person operating the setter would then give the plant a squirt of water by pulling on a small lever, open and lift the setter away from the plant, and then use their feet to compact the soil around the plant. The process was then repeated until the whole tobacco patch was set out – usually taking about two days.

Not long after being set out, the tobacco had to be tended by hoeing, chopping weeds, and spraying.

Keeping the weeds out of the tobacco patch seemed like a never-ending job. During rainy periods, the weeds would appear and grow faster than we could plow them under or chop them down.

I still remember the time our tobacco patch was near the barn. When plowing the tobacco and heading away from the barn, we would almost have to hit the horse to get him to move. But as soon as we started back toward the barn, the horse would really move, sometimes almost running. I am sure he was thinking that this time, he might get to quit pulling the plow and go into the barn for something to eat. His disappointment was obvious when we would make him turn around and head back the other way.

As the tobacco plants matured and began blooming, we had to top them by breaking off the blooms. After topping, suckers would grow between the leaves and have to be pulled off to prevent their continued growth - we called it suckering the tobacco. That always turned out to be a messy job because the tobacco juice was sticky like tar and difficult to get off our hands. We found that homemade lye soap was about the only thing that would really take it off.

During dry seasons, Dad worried a lot about our crops and could only watch as the leaves began to shrivel and the ground started cracking from the lack of rain.

But eventually, the rains would come, and the crops would quickly recover and begin growing again, although the yield was likely reduced if the dry spell had been really long.

As did other tasks associated with raising tobacco, cutting the tobacco involved a lot of bending, stooping, and lifting. The heavy stalks were cut off near the ground, below all leaves, and then lifted over the head and speared onto tobacco sticks. Most of the time, six stalks would fill each tobacco stick.

Most people, after a couple of days of cutting the tobacco, became really proficient at it. They could bend over, cut a heavy tobacco stalk, and then stand up straight and spear it onto the sticks in one continuous motion, almost without even looking at the sharp spear.

After cutting tobacco all day, no one complained about only having beans and cornbread again for supper, as long as there was plenty of it.

The cut tobacco was left in the field for a couple of days to wilt down and lose some weight, making it easier to handle. The tobacco was then hauled to the barn and hung on tobacco tiers until completely dry, which usually took a couple of months.

It was always a dangerous, hot job hanging tobacco in the barn to cure. It required someone to be high up near the tin roof of the barn, with the tobacco blocking airflow. Sweat from the uppermost person would drip down on those working below.

Tobacco Tier Poles Positioned and Ready in the Barn for Sticks of Tobacco (photo from Wikimedia Commons)

The dangerous part of the job was that someone had to be twenty feet high, straddling tier poles spaced about four feet apart. That person then had to walk backwards as they hung tobacco on the tier poles. Weight on the tier poles increased as each section was filled. The tier poles could break or slide, causing the person standing on them to fall and possibly hit others on the way down - or they hoped they would hit someone, as it might slow their fall.

Billy and I were lighter than the others and could climb like squirrels, so we usually were the ones highest up in the barn.

In addition to the risk of falling, wasp nests were always near the barn roof. Being that high up in the barn, and standing on slippery tier poles fighting wasps with sweat practically blinding us, was definitely a memorable event.

The tobacco remained in the barn drying for around two months, before we stripped the leaves into three or four grades and tied them into bundles using one of the leaves as a restraining band.

Stripping went much faster when enough people were helping such that one person was available for each grade of tobacco. Average-size tobacco patches of around one-half acre could be stripped in this manner in three or four full days.

Finally, around Thanksgiving, the tobacco was loaded onto a truck, taken to a tobacco auction, and sold. We always enjoyed watching the tobacco leave the farm. However, it was not long before we had to start the whole process over again.

As soon as Dad received the money from the sale of the tobacco, he would visit the grocery and other hardware or fertilizer stores where he owed money, and pay off his debts.

We would spend the short time between selling the tobacco in December to beginning preparation of the bed for next year's tobacco seeds in January or February by cleaning up the barn, replacing weak or broken tiers, and, if needed, making tobacco sticks to replace those lost or broken over the last year or two. When cared for, tobacco sticks lasted almost indefinitely, with some being handed down from generation to generation.

Although most people who raised tobacco smoked, I never saw anyone smoke homegrown tobacco. I often wondered why they didn't grind up the cured leaves and roll their own cigarettes, much as they did with store-bought tobacco, and save a lot of money.

Apparently, it was because commercial cigarette tobacco was a blend of different tobaccos from different regions to achieve a unique flavor. Smokers would develop a preference for particular flavors, or brands, such as Marlboro and Lucky Strike. The homegrown single type of unblended tobacco was not as flavorful.

Cigarette smokers, especially those in rural areas, seldom bought commercial packs of machine-rolled cigarettes, but would save money by buying loose tobacco and rolling their own cigarettes. The tobacco came in small cloth bags that held enough tobacco to roll about 30 cigarettes and cost 10 cents. A pack of 20 machine-rolled cigarettes cost 15 cents. Papers for rolling the cigarettes were included with the bags.

The little bags had a drawstring to reclose the bag after each cigarette. Machines were not available to thread the strings through the tops of the bags, so that part of the bag construction process had to be completed by hand.

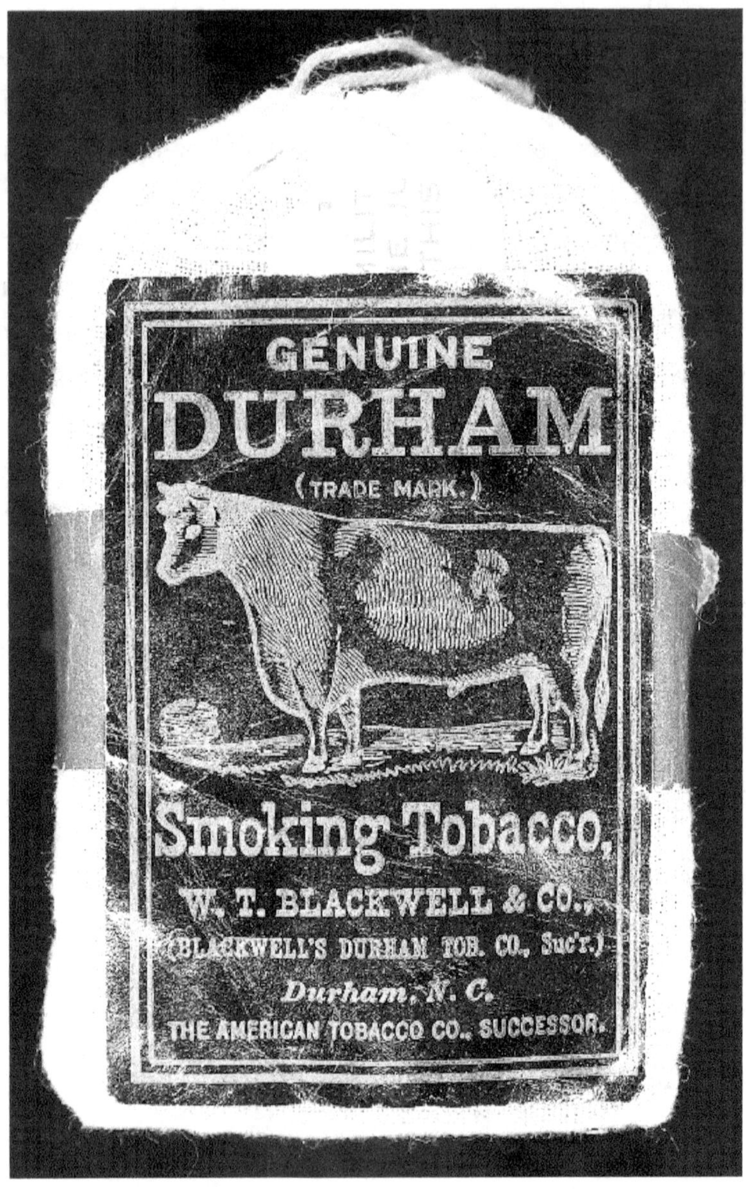

Cloth Tobacco Bag (photo from Wikimedia Commons)

During the Great Depression, many people in the Appalachian Mountains earned up to 50 cents a day threading the

drawstrings into the tops of the bags. Some people became really proficient at this and could thread as many as a thousand bags a day.

The empty tobacco bags had many other uses. Mom would store coins and other small items in the bags. They were also just the right size for storing garden seeds such as watermelon and cantaloupe (we always called cantaloupes mush melons).

Caught Smoking

My cousin Leroy and I used to experiment with smoking. We tried everything, including rabbit tobacco, which was a weed that grew in our fields, wild grapevines, and just about anything else we could set afire and make smoke.

Smoking grapevines was easy because they have a hollow stem. All one had to do was cut a section of vine about four inches long, light it, and begin puffing. Depending on how green the vine was, the taste would vary from terrible, including burning the lips, to almost tolerable with a slight sweet taste.

I don't know why we even did it, as everything we tried, including real tobacco, tasted awful and usually made us cough and sick.

One day, we were sitting behind my uncle's barn trying some of the partly cured tobacco that had been drying for at least a month. We didn't have the thin cigarette papers, so, as usual, we just used old newspaper to roll the tobacco into cigarettes.

Just as we started having a big time laughing and trying to be the first to inhale without coughing, Leroy's dad, my uncle Ervin, walked around the corner of the barn and up to us. I expected a good chewing out, but all he said to us was "Hello,

Boys", and kept on going. It was obvious he saw us smoking, but said nothing about it.

Days went by, and he still hadn't said anything about catching us smoking. We figured he was waiting to tell my dad so we both could be punished at the same time. We kept imagining how bad it was going to be and just wished he would say something and get it over with.

We talked about asking if he was going to do something. I was getting tired of looking at Mom and Dad's faces every time I came into the house, to see if they were mad and ready to mete out some punishment.

This went on for at least two weeks, and we finally decided he wasn't planning to tell anyone. But we worried about it for at least another two or three months.

To this day, I don't know whether he intentionally didn't say anything as his way of punishment, or just forgot about it.

Intentional or not, I believe all the worrying about it was the right punishment, as I never again smoked another cigarette of any kind. Actually, I never even came close to wanting to try another one. I don't know whether Leroy ever became a smoker, but I never saw him smoking.

Until 1938, burley tobacco production was unregulated, meaning each farmer was allowed to grow as much of it as they wanted. Farmers increased the amount of tobacco they grew, causing prices and profits to fall. That resulted in a vicious cycle of further increasing their production causing prices to fall even further. After a while, the prices were so low, the farmers were barely recovering their costs.

In order to stabilize prices and ensure the farmers could receive a decent return on their efforts, the Government began assigning tobacco bases to each farm. Any amount planted over their base had to be destroyed. By 2004, health concerns reduced the demand for tobacco to the point that the government enacted a buyout program to again stabilize prices. Most small farmers sold their tobacco bases back to the government and stopped growing tobacco altogether.

13

Chickens and Molasses Don't Mix

We seldom bought treats such as ice cream, Cokes, or candy, so we made our own goodies. We either made or helped in making the treats, and Mom always had to clean up the mess we left behind. She probably cringed each time we decided to make something.

Sassafras Tea

Sassafras bushes and trees were common in our area, and especially so at and near our Big Clifty home. The leaves of the sassafras tree resemble mittens and are the most easily recognized of nearly any tree.

Sassafras roots have a distinct sweet smell, sort of like a combination of root beer and vanilla, making them very easy to distinguish from other roots.

This unique smell and taste are what made sassafras commercially popular for teas, root beer, and other products. However, the root and its oils were banned in 1960 due to the potential carcinogenic effects. Now, it is only used in a few specialty candies and for personal use. Some niche foods use an extract from the root but not the oils.

We would dig the roots of young small sassafras saplings because they were the easiest to dig and smelled especially strong. When breaking the root of these saplings, the pleasant smell was immediately recognizable.

I don't know what would cause us to think of digging some for tea, but I guess it was just something to do. We would grab a shovel or hoe and maybe an axe and head for an area we knew had sassafras bushes. Sassafras grew well in fence rows and at the edge of woods.

It didn't take long to dig a few roots and head back to the house.

We would wash them and then boil several in a pot of water. We never got the same strength of tea twice because we had no idea how many roots to put in the pot or for how long. We just threw in a few roots and covered them with water. Almost immediately, the water would start turning a light reddish color. After boiling the roots for a few minutes, we would sweeten the tea and drink it hot.

At least a few times, we accidentally got the strength about right, and the resulting tea tasted pretty good. However, most of the time, we would take a sip of the tea and then pour out the rest. It was usually either much too strong or too weak.

Snow Ice Cream

During the winters, we looked forward to the first snowfall so we could make our own "snow ice cream."

As soon as the first snow started accumulating, we would run outside and use spoons to scrape up a bowlful. We usually couldn't wait for the snow to get deep enough to ensure we scraped up only snow. Sometimes we picked up tree bark, leaves, and even dirt along with the snow.

Mom always cautioned us to be careful and not pick up yellow-looking snow, as it might be stained that way by animal urine.

After bringing it inside, we first tried picking out most of the contaminants we had picked up along with the snow. Our snow ice cream was then made by mixing the snow with milk, vanilla, and a little sugar. As I remember, it actually tasted good, and we would eat our fill.

The first time I remember tasting real ice cream was when I was around 14. A friend and I had been helping a neighbor cut tobacco. After quitting for the day, we were each paid two or three dollars and we decided to go to a nearby store and use some of our money to buy ice cream.

We had been planning to buy just a small ice cream bar each, but the much larger half-gallon box sizes of ice cream were now available and kept drawing our attention. We reasoned that we could buy a whole half-gallon for about the same price as two bars. We finally decided to go with a half-gallon of vanilla ice cream, eat some ourselves, and then divide the rest of it to take home to our siblings.

That plan didn't work out because after stopping on the way home to eat our share, we just kept eating one more spoonful until it was all gone.

Eating the whole thing apparently didn't make either of us sick - maybe because we were practically starved from cutting tobacco all day.

I felt a little guilty about not taking some home to the others, but got over that feeling pretty quickly by rationalizing that it would have most likely melted before we could get there anyway. By eating it, we were actually saving the others from being disappointed by finding it completely melted.

Popcorn Balls

Most years, we planted a row or two of popcorn in the garden. After gathering the ears of corn and letting them dry, we would shell them by hand and store the popcorn grains in gallon jars.

We popped the corn using a long-handled popcorn popper held over a hot stove. All of us, including Juanita, would want to hold the popper while the corn popped and, as usual, argued about who would hold it first. Juanita, being very young, would stand on a chair and try to hold the hot handle of the popper. It didn't take her long to decide to wait until the corn was popped.

Quite often, one of us would actually get burned and spill the corn, but the next time we went through the same arguments again over who would be first in holding the popper.

After popping the corn, we heated the sorghum molasses and poured it over the popped corn. We then rubbed butter on our hands to keep the molasses from sticking to us and squeezed handfuls of corn and sorghum into large balls. I wish I could remember if we washed our hands first, but I am guessing we did not.

Although they were a real treat to eat, they usually remained sticky even after cooling. Our sticky fingers left a lot of fingerprints all over us, the furniture, and the rest of the house.

The good thing about popcorn balls was that you could take them outside and eat them while playing or hunting. We probably ate a lot of things we didn't intend to, as we would lay them down wherever it was convenient and then pick them up and continue eating.

Natural Treats

In addition to our homemade treats, nature provided us with several tasty items that only needed to be picked or cracked.

For instance, in the summer, there were lots of blackberries and dew berries that we would eat right off the vine or cover with milk and sugar. We would also find patches of wild blueberries and raspberries, and occasionally a tree with ripe mulberries. All the berries would stain our hands, face, and clothes, but the stain went away after a few days.

During the fall, there were plenty of hickory nuts, walnuts, and hazelnuts. Just before frost, we would look for wild grapes, persimmons, and crabapples.

Fully ripe persimmons tasted great, but we would dare each other to take a bite of green persimmons or green crabapples and then try to talk. Both of these would make our tongues and lips curl up, causing us to spit them out.

Homemade Hominy

We sometimes made hominy in a large, cast-iron kettle over an outside fire. It was fairly easy to make from mature dry corn and a helping of lye to loosen the hard corn hulls.

If we were out of store-bought lye, Mom would make a homemade version by pouring water over wood ashes.

Chickens and Molasses Don't Mix

We grew sugarcane for a couple of years, using it to make sorghum (we called it molasses). After the molasses were made, we stored them in five-gallon lard cans on the back porch, where they stayed relatively cool.

One summer, someone dipped molasses out of one of the cans on the porch but did not properly replace the lid. A hen came onto the porch, jumped onto the loose lid, and fell into the molasses can. The more she struggled, the deeper she sank as if in quicksand.

When discovered, her head was barely above the molasses, but the rest of her body was completely submerged and immobilized. Mom was so mad at the hen for ruining the molasses that she wanted to jerk her out of the can by the neck. But, she thought better of it and tried to save the hen by lifting her out and then trying to wash the molasses off. She was able to get some of the molasses off the hen, but it was so thick and sticky that much of it would not come off.

Probably the only thing that would have worked was to pull out all her feathers, but I doubt the chicken would have liked that very much.

I don't remember what happened to her after that. Mom likely just turned her loose to let the molasses wear off, or maybe a fox enjoyed a tasty molasses-covered, sweet-tasting chicken.

Molasses is made by boiling sugarcane juice until all water is removed, leaving a thick, rich, dark syrup. Ten gallons of juice are required to make one gallon of molasses.

We looked forward to the cane ripening so we could suck the juice directly from the stalk. We would cut down several stalks and either suck the juice right there in the cane patch or take them to a nearby shade tree to get out of the hot sun.

We would strip off the leaves and then bite into the stalks several times to split the tough green outer shell. We would then hold the stalk in our mouths and twist it to force out the sweet juice. We had to be careful when biting the stalks to keep from cutting our lips and tongues.

Sometimes, we would peel the bark off the stalk and chew the soft inner core of the cane to get at the juice. The leftover core was then spit out.

When the cane was fully mature, we would strip the leaves from the standing stalks and then cut the cane near the ground using a machete-like knife. The cane stalks were then loaded on a truck and hauled to my Granddad's Molasses Mill, which was set up at his farm in White Mills.

A mule or a horse walked in a tight circle, turning the mill as cane stalks were fed into it and crushed, squeezing out the juice. The person feeding the canes into the mill sat close to the mill and below the height of the turning arm being pulled and rotated by the horse.

Juice from the mill was collected in buckets and poured into a large, shallow metal pan sitting over a hot wood fire. The juice was then boiled for several hours with almost continuous stirring to prevent it from burning. As impurities rose to the surface, they were skimmed off. The hot fire gradually evaporated the water from the cane juice, causing it to thicken and eventually become molasses.

The fire had to be really hot, so most of the boiling was accomplished at night to avoid the heat of the day. I stayed and watched the whole thing and maybe even helped a little by moving the crushed stalks out of the way. I remember having to duck the long pole each time the horse made a complete circle.

I began sampling the juice as soon as it became hot and kept at it as it slowly changed in color and consistency, growing darker and more syrupy as the water kept boiling off. Finally, after hours of boiling, stirring, and sampling, what remained in the pan was pure molasses—thick, sticky, and flavorful.

We gave my granddad at least a 5-gallon lard can full of molasses and still had plenty left to take home for ourselves.

The crushed canes were also taken back home and scattered over the field to enrich the soil.

14

Juanita Gets a Tricycle

My sister Juanita was about four years old when Billy and I decided she needed a tricycle. Each of us boys had something that at least resembled a bicycle, but all she could do was watch us ride around in the yard.

We asked a local grocery store owner what we could do to earn enough money to buy a tricycle. He suggested we dig and sell Mayapple roots, as it was then around the middle of May, and Mayapple was abundant along road banks and at the edges of woods.

The store owner regularly hauled livestock to the Louisville stock market, and he agreed to take the roots with him and sell them for us. He suggested we might get 25 cents a pound, but they had to be dry.

Mayapple roots had been used as a laxative by American Indians for hundreds of years, and were a principal ingredient in Carter's Little Liver Pills that had been aggressively marketed in the 1940s and 50's.

The roots are still used as medicine in the treatment of warts and in some cancer therapies.

Mayapple patches were spread throughout our uncle's nearby woods, with most growing in loose soil, making the roots easy to uncover.

Mayapple Patch

We worked for at least two full days until we had a large pile that looked as if we had enough to buy a car, not just a tricycle. But, we wanted to make sure we had enough roots and hopefully have some money left over for us.

We knocked as much dirt off the roots as we could, and then put them into four or five large grass sacks. After we got the roots home, we washed off the dirt and left them in the sun to dry. A couple of days later, the roots were much lighter and seemed dry enough. We bagged them up and took them to the grocery store owner, anxious for our big payday. At 25 cents a pound, we were surely going to have plenty of money left over.

He took one look at them and told us he couldn't sell them unless we dried them first. He went on to explain that they had to be dry on the inside as well as the outside, which would take at least 2 or 3 months, not days.

We took the roots back home and this time, spread them out on the floor of an unused upstairs room in our house. We had so many roots, they covered the entire floor, two or three inches deep.

Every week or two, we would stir the pile to make sure the roots at the bottom were also getting dry. After a few weeks of drying, they had shrunk drastically and were at least five times lighter than before. We began to believe feathers would be heavier than our roots.

We sacked them up again and once more took them to the store owner. This time, however, we were able to get all of them into one grass sack weighing maybe 15 or 20 pounds. We had been expecting to get rich, but now we were hoping we had enough to buy the tricycle. We received a little over four dollars, which was really close to what a tricycle cost at that time. I don't remember how we actually got the tricycle, but

Dad must have bought it in Leitchfield and pitched in the difference between our four dollars and whatever the tricycle actually cost.

Dad Pretending to Ride Juanita's Tricycle

When he first brought it home, Dad pretended to ride the tricycle and told Juanita we had bought it for him. She knew better since we had been talking about it and messing with the Mayapple roots all summer.

She must have learned to ride it on the porch or inside the house because there weren't many smooth surfaces outside. Our driveway was graveled, and the yard was pretty rough from clumps of grass and the dogs digging in it all the time.

All parts of the Mayapple plant are poisonous, except the fruit can be eaten - but only when fully ripe and then only in moderation. Even the roots are poisonous, which is why they are useful as laxatives and for removing warts when correctly used and in small dosages.

Since we didn't know the plants were poisonous, Billy somehow got the idea that the tops of the Mayapple plant might make good feed for the hogs. He tested his theory by giving an armload of the green tops to a couple of sow hogs Dad was fattening up to kill in the fall.

The hogs seemed to really like them, and Billy was about ready to announce finding a new and abundant food source for the hogs. But both hogs suddenly died before he had the opportunity to tell anyone the good news.

He then decided to keep that good news to himself, leaving Dad trying to figure out what happened to his hogs.

I am almost certain Billy was wise to withhold that particular information.

15

Doug Had a Mind of His Own

When Doug was around seven or eight years old, he was always catching frogs, lizards, or grasshoppers and playing with them while forgetting what he was supposed to be doing.

Keeping Doug on the Job

One season, tobacco worms were really harming our tobacco. They are so large that they are easy to see on the tobacco leaves, so the easiest and most effective way to get rid of them is to pick them off and smash them against the ground or just stomp on them.

Doug eventually became old enough to help pick off the worms. Being small, he was actually better able than Billy or I to spot the tobacco worms on the lower leaves.

The problem was that he was easily distracted by a lot of things other than the worms he was supposed to be catching.

The tobacco was taller than any of us, so Billy and I couldn't see him, but we would keep up with him by listening as he turned over the tobacco leaves looking for worms. But when things got really quiet, we knew we had better start looking for him because more than likely, he had turned his attention away from hunting tobacco worms and was on the trail of something more interesting to him. We would search for him and return him to his workstation, only to have to do it again about five minutes later.

Keeping Doug on course with the tobacco worms was hard enough, but occasionally, we would be cutting wood or doing some other work away from the house and become terribly thirsty. We always knew better, but would still send Doug to the house for water. We always hoped he would not see anything interesting during his trip.

But he usually did, and would be gone for what seemed forever. By the time he got back to us, we were about to die of thirst, and usually, most of the water had been spilled or left at some crawdad hole near the pond. We would ask him where the water was, and he would say "oh" and head back toward the house again.

Trouble in the Apple Orchard

Doug demonstrated his temper and ability to hold a grudge more than once. A neighbor owned an apple orchard located about two miles from our Big Clifty home, and told Mom we could have all the apples we wanted. Mom sent Doug and me to pick up about a bushel of them off the ground so she could can them. At that time, we had a small wagon that was big enough to hold at least a bushel and could be easily pulled by hand. We sometimes also used the wagon when we were hunting for black walnuts or hickory nuts.

We fooled around on the way, but eventually got there and began picking up apples. We had the wagon about half full when a man who lived a little farther down the road from the orchard came walking by and started chewing us out for getting the apples.

I don't know if it was true or not, but we had heard tales that years ago, he had killed his daughter with a pitchfork. The story may have had some basis in fact, but the killing part may have grown a bit in retelling it. But he definitely had a reputation for being mean to his kids.

Because of the stories, I was a little afraid of him, but I tried to explain that we had the landowner's permission to get the apples. That didn't seem to make a difference to the guy, and he just kept on saying we were stealing the apples and we better leave them alone.

The stories about the pitchfork didn't intimidate Doug, who was only nine or ten years old. Doug spoke up and told the man to go on home because they weren't his apples, and anyway, we were going to get all we wanted. The guy kept saying he might call the law on us.

When he saw we were not leaving without the apples, he finally went on his way.

He must have been planning to get the apples himself; otherwise, he surely wouldn't have been so agitated over us collecting the apples, and especially since he knew who we were.

I cautioned Doug not to say anything about this to Dad or Mom because it would just cause problems.

I had nearly forgotten about the incident, but about three months later, he came to our house to borrow a tool.

I didn't say anything to him about the earlier incident and was willing to drop the matter altogether. But Doug saw him while Dad was talking to him, and immediately got between him and Dad, and right up in the man's face, and dared him to say the same things to us now that he said in the apple orchard. That was brave talk from a nine-year-old kid to a grown man that we believed had killed his daughter.

The man became nervous and muttered that he was kidding us and didn't know we would take it seriously. But Doug didn't back down and kept on daring him to repeat what he had said to us in the orchard.

Dad was caught off guard by Doug's attack and told him to back off, and we would talk about it later. I did notice Dad did not loan the guy whatever he had wanted to borrow.

After he had gone, Dad asked us what was going on. I downplayed the episode because I was still concerned Dad or Mom would do or say something they would regret. Dad believed us, but probably felt the whole incident may have been blown a little out of proportion. He said to forget about it this time, but be sure and tell him if anything like that ever happens again.

Neither Dad, Doug, nor I ever mentioned the incident to Mom. Mom was always even-tempered and friendly to everybody, but she had a temper – probably where Doug got his and would show it if someone tried to take advantage of her, or if she got mad enough. No doubt, she would have gone after the guy like a mother bear defending her young.

I sometimes regret not backing Doug up rather than trying to downplay the incident. But maybe it was the best approach after all, as the incident was never mentioned again, and we never had another encounter with the guy. He had a son who was a few years older than Doug and me, and we remained good friends for years afterward.

Doug Goes Off Fishing - Again

Doug was only eight or ten years old, but often sneaked off by himself to go fishing in the creek at the Rock House. When he wouldn't show back up after two or three hours, Mom would really begin to worry, and a little later would have convinced herself that he had fallen over the cliff or fallen in the creek and drowned.

She actually had good reason to worry, because there were a lot of ways to get hurt or even killed near the Rock House, especially for a small kid by himself. Unless really careful, one could fall while descending the steep hill to the Rock House, trip and go over a vertical rock cliff, or actually slip and fall into the creek. The creek usually wasn't deep enough in most places to worry about, but someone could easily hit their head on large rocks as they fell in.

I would tell her not to worry because he does this all the time. He gets interested in fishing or hunting grasshoppers and pays no attention to the time. I would tell her to wait at least another hour, and I bet he is back.

That explanation never worked because the last time he was in trouble for going off alone, he had promised her that he would not go there by himself again, but if he did, he would only stay a short while. As only a mother would, she actually believed him.

Then I would try a different approach to get out of having to go all the way to the Rock House. I would remind her how far it was, and how he may not be there anyway. He could have gone to a friend's house or been back the other direction picking blackberries or something, and we would be going all that distance for nothing. I would try convincing her that while we were gone looking for him, he would probably come home and be playing in the yard when we got back. That approach didn't work either.

She was always insistent and unable to just wait to see if he came home. So, she would walk with me at least a half mile, all the way to the top of the hill above the rock house. On the way, she would keep thinking and muttering about all the ways he probably had gotten hurt and if he hadn't gotten hurt or killed, he was going to wish he had.

By the time we got to the top of the hill, she had totally convinced herself that the only possible reason he hadn't come home was that he was hurt badly or maybe dead. She would then stay at the top of the hill while I went the rest of the way down the wooded and rugged hill and searched for Doug. She stayed there because she couldn't stand the thought of seeing his body floating in the creek.

I can imagine her worry while I was gone, because it would take me at least 25 minutes to descend the hill, follow the creek a short distance to the Rock House, and then climb back up. If he wasn't there, then I would be gone much longer, as I would have to go up and down the creek looking for him.

It was a steep hill, and going down to the creek wasn't easy. While going down, I was always hoping he was at least close to where he usually fished and hadn't wandered the opposite direction up the creek.

Sure enough, once I had made it down to the creek, I would find him sitting on the creek bank having a good ole time fishing. He would ask, "What are you doing here?" which made me mad - I felt like just shoving him into the creek.

I would explain to him that Mom was waiting for me to bring his body back up to the top of the hill, and since he wasn't dead, she was going to skin him alive.

Mom was always so relieved to see that he was okay; she would completely forget about punishing him. Doug would promise not to do it again, but true to his nature, about a month later, he would.

16

Local Grocery Stores

Small Mom & Pop grocery stores used to be located every few miles along main roads and at major intersections. Most of those were owned and operated by someone who lived nearby and was well known in the community. The stores generally went by the owner's name, and the owners knew everyone who regularly patronized their store. There may have been franchise or chain groceries in towns, but none in rural areas such as ours.

By today's standards, our local grocery stores were nothing more than oversized pantries. In fact, Kroger today probably has more shelf space for cereal alone than our local stores had for everything, including chicken feed and cattle salt blocks. Still, those small stores were perfectly adequate and served the needs of the surrounding community.

All stores carried only one or two brands of each item, unlike large grocery stores of today that may carry 50 varieties or brands of the same item. There was no point in stocking a dozen varieties of the same product when two or three brands were plenty. Rural folks were creatures of habit, loyal to their favorites, and the store owner knew it. His job wasn't to overwhelm us with choices, but to make sure the shelves held exactly what the community wanted—no more, no less.

Most stores looked much the same, including overall physical size. They were usually about the size of a small house with a public retail area and a backroom for storage. Many had a few chairs sitting on the front porch for folks to hang out and talk for a few minutes before going in and getting their groceries. Most had a cola dispenser sitting on the front porch or just inside the door with different brands of colas hanging by their bottle necks. Colas were a nickel each.

A single gas pump, with leaded regular gasoline, and a kerosene tank were in front of the store. If you needed gas or kerosene, the store owner came outside and pumped it for you. Self-service gas stations were far in the future. Premium gasoline did not become generally available until years later, when car engines became much more powerful and had higher cylinder compression. Those newer engines required gasoline with a higher octane to avoid pre-ignition and engine knocking.

The store owners typically did not provide other attentive services, like most regular gas stations, because they barely had time to pump the fuel.

We never bought more than one or two dollars' worth of gas at a time, which at the then price of 29 cents/gallon, would buy from three to five gallons. That was enough for several short trips to the store and around the community. We never filled up the car with gas, even when on long trips to visit my grandparents in the mountains. Maybe that was so we could use the restrooms while gas was being pumped.

I was in the eighth grade before seeing someone get a gas fill-up. It was so unusual that it made a lasting impression on me, and I remember who it was, which store it was purchased from, and which side of the pump the car was sitting on when it was filled up. I am not sure I knew that car gas tanks could be filled.

Inside the store, shelves of groceries lined the walls. Most of the time, the store owner stayed behind counters that served as a display shelf and a place for larger or heavier items.

One either told the store owner what was wanted or most often simply handed them a list of needed items. I believe we wrote out a list of needed items because we often walked to the grocery store, and certainly didn't want to have to make another trip just because we forgot a key item. Also, one could be looking around at other things while the store owner filled the list.

Most lists, including ours, were usually short and included only those basic items such as flour, cornmeal, sugar, coffee, and salt. Those were the items that we needed but did not grow or make ourselves.

As with gas stations, self-service grocery shopping was not yet even envisioned.

Most of the store's items were not marked with a price. You usually asked the price of things you didn't normally buy. The owner knew the price, or if not, could look it up on a price list.

The store owner would pick the items from the shelves, ring them up on the cash register, and bag them, ready to be handed to the customer. I don't remember us ever buying over $5 worth of groceries at one time, which usually filled one or two large brown grocery bags.

Scanners and barcodes had not yet been invented, so there was no such thing as auto-re-ordering after an item was sold. The owner simply looked at his shelves and decided which items he needed to restock once the delivery truck arrived.

Generally, people didn't care what brand of sugar they got, so the store would usually need to stock only one brand of sugar. However, most people did develop a preference for some products, such as a particular brand of coffee, so the store would usually need to stock two or three brands of those products, including, for instance, Maxwell House and American Ace. If someone preferred a particular brand but it was not carried by the store, the owner would stock it for a while to see if there was sufficiently long-term demand for it.

The colorful cloth flour sacks were designed for later use in making shirts and other clothing items. Sometimes, Mom would switch to a different brand of flour because she liked the particular color and design of sacks.

We never bought milk, bread, eggs, potatoes, butter, nor canned goods such as green beans and tomatoes. These and lots of other food items were home-grown rather than bought. We did occasionally buy bologna when we were working away from home. We usually had plenty of milk to drink and to use in cooking and for making cream and butter.

We made our own butter by first separating the cream from raw milk and then churning the cream for about 30 minutes until the butter formed. The butter was removed, and the remaining liquid was buttermilk, which we would either drink or use in making buttermilk cornbread.

We would sometimes put the cream into a half-gallon jar and vigorously shake it until the butter formed, rather than use a churn. That usually took at least 15 minutes with two people taking turns shaking the jar of cream. We would sell the leftover cream to the local store along with any excess eggs.

The grocery store served a need somewhat like credit cards do today. Most people, including us, didn't always have cash or sufficient bank checking accounts to immediately pay for groceries. We had to buy groceries on credit until we sold an animal, such as a hog, or sold our primary cash crop, tobacco.

When we didn't have the cash, we would tell the grocery store owner to "Put it on the books," which meant charge it. The store owner maintained a book with the names of all those regular customers whom the owner allowed to buy on credit and would add the amount to the list. As soon as we had the cash, we would have the owner total the list, and we would pay some or all of the charges.

The store owners almost always knew the kids of their regular customers, and thus they were allowed to make normal purchases and charge them to their parents' accounts.

Many people, including us, would make their own cornmeal by shelling yellow or white field corn and having it ground into meal at the local mill. That way, we rarely needed to purchase commercially ground cornmeal.

I have fond memories of shelling corn to be ground into cornmeal. We would shell at night by placing a large tub in the middle of the floor, and everyone would sit around it and shell the corn by hand. We didn't do that very often, so it was always a novel activity for us kids. I doubt we were careful about what went into the tub. It usually took a while to shell a tub full of corn, often winding up with blisters on our hands.

We owned a hand-cranked corn Sheller, but we never used it when we were shelling corn for cornmeal. We only used it when shelling corn for chickens and sometimes for the milk cows. It may have allowed too much corn cob and other undesirable stuff to be mixed into the shelled corn.

The shelled corn was poured into one or two large burlap sacks and taken to the mill in Big Clifty for grinding into cornmeal.

The milling process was always interesting to watch as the corn was ground between two large flat stones. Sometimes the meal would be ground too coarse and have to be reground. I don't remember what we stored the ground cornmeal in, but it may have been sacks supplied by the mill.

The mill and grinding stones were most often used for grinding corn into animal feed. I suppose the grinding stones were cleaned before grinding our cornmeal, but I am not sure.

Occasionally, we would run out of our own ground cornmeal and buy a sack at the grocery. I remember Mom would get really disgusted and fuss when she opened the cornmeal and found weevils in it. This happened quite often because of the fairly low turnover rate of some items at the grocery store, particularly cornmeal. She would always take it back at the first opportunity, and swap it for another sack and hope it didn't have weevils. If that one also had weevils, she would swear she was never going to that store again. But after getting cornmeal free of weevils, she would forget all about threatening to quit buying from that store, and everything was good until she found weevils in another sack of cornmeal.

The grocery store owners always got the blame for the weevils, but more than likely, weevil eggs were already in the corn when it was ground and packaged. By the time the corn-meal was purchased and opened, the eggs had time to hatch into weevils.

17

The Garden Queen

Everyone in our rural area, including us, raised a garden to supply fresh vegetables during the summer and canned food during the winter. Large, well-cared-for gardens were a matter of pride. When passing someone's home, you always looked at their garden and mentally compared it to your own. Gardens that were really small or neglected with lots of weeds reflected poorly on their owners.

Mom took ownership of our gardens because she knew how important they were in providing year-round food for the family. She would make sure the weeds didn't take it, or bugs didn't eat more than their share. She also made sure we planted the right mix of vegetables, and everything was cared for from planting through harvest.

She always saved the best seeds from last year's plants, such as watermelons and beans, but purchased seeds for small-seeded plants, such as tomatoes and turnips.

She did a lot of the lighter work, such as planting and hoeing herself, but drafted us for the heavier work, including plowing, digging potatoes, and carrying produce into the house.

Each year, we raised both regular and sweet potatoes, tomatoes, onions, sweet corn, lots of beans, okra, lettuce, and whatever other seeds or plants we could find.

For at least a couple of years, we planted a row or two of peanuts, and, as I remember, they did fairly well. They were quite tasty after roasting them in the oven. I don't know if we were tired of them or what, but we stopped planting them after those couple of years. It may have been that we got carried away and ate our seed peanuts, and after a while, forgot all about them.

For some reason, we always purchased seed potatoes. Maybe the ones we had left over from last year's crop were affected by the winter weather and would not produce healthy potatoes. The seed potatoes were cut into small sections, with each section containing at least one potato eye, which would sprout and form the potato plant.

As soon as the new potatoes began to form and grow, we would dig into the hills, checking their size, anxious to make a thick soup from the starchy new potatoes.

In the fall, after the potato vines had died back, we would dig the potatoes with shovels or occasionally a single plow pulled by one of our horses. We would pick up the potatoes, put them into grass sacks, and store them in the crib or smoke-house. It was always fun to find odd-shaped or large potatoes.

One year, Dad and Mom planted several rows of potatoes in what had been our hog lot for many years. The ground was fertile because the hogs had kept it loosened up and well fertilized.

The hog lot potatoes grew exceptionally well and produced so many potatoes that they completely covered our smokehouse floor, nearly a foot deep.

Word spread, and our neighbors would visit to see the large amount of potatoes we had gotten from the small area of the hog lot. I don't remember what we did with them, but I did hear Dad talking about possibly digging a large hole and burying a bunch of them in straw to see if they would keep over winter. Likely, the vast majority of them were just given away or traded for something else.

Mom would sometimes plant a short row of lettuce for making salads. We would heat bacon or sausage grease to nearly boiling, and then pour it over the lettuce. We would also add a generous helping of salt, making the salad quite tasty. The combination probably wasn't very healthy for us.

We would occasionally have poke greens with a meal by picking the young, tender leaves of pokeweed—that we simply called *poke salad*—and boiling them much like we did turnip greens. Pokeweed grew wild around our farm, especially in rich spots like old dirt piles, fence rows, and near half-rotten stumps.

We didn't realize then that pokeweed can be poisonous unless it's thoroughly cooked and rinsed two or three times. I doubt we were that careful with it, but as far as I know, we never suffered any harm from eating it.

Our tobacco bed, being protected by a canvas cover, was the perfect place to start tomato plants so they'd be ready to set out as soon as the danger of frost had passed. Mom would sow the tomato seeds in the tobacco bed, and once the young plants reached eight or ten inches tall, we'd transplant them into the garden.

As soon as the young tomatoes appeared, we would begin checking them, anxious to have the first ripe tomatoes. We really enjoyed picking the tomatoes off the vine and eating them right there in the garden. I would dip the tomato into a handful of salt I had brought with me to the tomato patch. That much salt was likely not a good thing, but although it didn't seem to have had an obvious, immediate harmful effect on me, it did create a lifelong tendency to over-salt my food.

Sweet corn was planted in rows by hand using a hand-held corn planter that had a small container to hold the seed corn. We would push the tip of the planter into the soft ground and then pull a trigger to release one or two grains of corn. We would then step on the hill of corn to make sure the corn seed was in good contact with the soil and move on to the next hill.

In the late 40's, we owned an old military jeep, and Billy used it a few times to disk our garden before planting. He couldn't get close enough into the corners of the garden, so we reverted to using horses for the disking job.

We spent a lot of time plowing and hoeing the garden to prevent the weeds from crowding out the young garden plants. Other regular garden jobs included staking the pole beans to provide support for the beans to grow upwards, dusting the potatoes with insecticide to help control potato bugs, and sometimes pinching off the ends of the watermelon vines. I still wonder if pinching off the watermelon vines actually helped in producing larger watermelons or was just a handed-down, unproven practice.

The real work of the garden fell on Mom's shoulders after everything started ripening. Beginning in August, the hottest time of the year, she would begin the seemingly never-ending job of canning the garden produce. We picked vegetables from the garden, and she would can them over a hot wood fire in the kitchen, without air conditioning or fans. She canned just about everything, including apples, peaches, blackberries, beets, beans, and tomatoes. She would usually end up with a total of about two hundred pint, quart, and half-gallon jars of food when done.

It was a busy time of the year for Mom. The vegetables and blackberries had to be picked at just the right time before getting too ripe, beans had to be strung and broken up, apples and peaches had to be gathered or bought and peeled.

Mom would often use a pressure cooker when canning. After putting the cans of food inside the pressure cooker, the lid was fastened down with several bolts and knobs. A small vent valve on top of the lid controlled the pressure inside the cooker by venting air and steam when the pressure rose above the set pressure.

Most pressure cookers had warnings pasted on them for the operators to make sure the vent valve was operating correctly; otherwise, the pressure cooker could blow up from excessive pressure. The vent valve would continually weave side to side while venting the built-up pressures. Until it started venting, she would worry that the valve might not be working because it was either in the wrong position or somehow broken.

Nearly all our neighbors had a story to tell about how someone they knew, or had heard of, was killed or had their house severely damaged when a pressure cooker exploded. It was obvious Mom was afraid of the pressure cooker because if she wasn't looking, and we dropped something, the unexpected noise would make her almost jump out of her skin. She would scold us never to do that again.

Pickles could be canned or prepared in several different ways. Our dill pickles were canned with just salt, dill, and water. Sweet pickles were soaked in vinegar, sugar, and spices for at least 14 days before canning.

August seemed to be the perfect storm of activity. Most of the garden canning work needed to be done at the same time our tobacco needed to be topped, suckered, and maybe even cut. In addition, hay needed to be cut and stored in the barn, and preparations for return to school had to be completed. I am sure it was difficult for Mom and Dad to decide which task was most important each day.

We didn't have a cellar or basement for storing the canned food, so it had to be distributed in available closets and on shelves throughout the warmer areas of the house, which were only the kitchen and living room. A lot of Mom's hard work was lost when cans of food would freeze and burst open in cold weather.

I don't remember exactly how it all got started, but for a while, it seems our whole community was talking about growing and selling pickles. Maybe a fast-talking salesman from the pickle industry had come through, promising easy money for anyone willing to plant cucumbers. Many nearby farmers were already familiar with growing a few hills of cucumbers in their gardens and knew how quickly they produced. It didn't take much imagination to picture the baskets of cucumbers they could gather from a much larger patch. Before long, several farmers decided to plant from a quarter-acre to a full acre, hoping to make quick and easy money.

What the salesman apparently failed to mention was the problems of growing pickles using nothing but manual labor. The biggest issue was that pickle buyers mostly wanted small pickles—they wouldn't pay much for the larger ones the farmers had in mind when planning to grow pickles. Since cucumbers grow fast, the only way to get a reasonable price per pound was to pick them every day. If even a day was missed, the small pickles quickly grew too large and were considered lower grade. That meant daily harvesting, even though the small pickles were lightweight, and required several to weigh a pound.

The work was back-breaking. Pickers had to move row by row, stooped over, searching through the vines for the small ones. It took hundreds of those little pickles just to fill a single basket, which then had to be hauled to the processing plant near E-town several times a week.

To make matters worse, weed control was nearly impossible because the vines spread between the rows, making it difficult when using a plow. After a couple of years of sore backs and little money, everyone gave up on growing pickles for sale.

One year, Dad decided we would set out a large patch of strawberries of about a half-acre. That would give us plenty of strawberries for our own use, with plenty left over to sell. However, the strawberry plan turned out to be a disaster, and we got no more than a bowl or two of strawberries – total. We had put the strawberry patch in a fairly low area, and that year we had excessive rain, which drowned out many of the plants. Even worse, the wet weather prevented us from plowing and hoeing the strawberries, allowing the weeds and grass to take over.

Dad considered getting several geese and seeing if they would stay in the strawberry patch and eat the grass. But, he finally decided that wouldn't work and just plowed everything under.

18

The Versatile Sears Roebuck Catalog

We were always glad to get the new Sears and Roebuck catalogs – we called them Wish Books. The catalog came early in the year, and then we would receive at least two addenda – one before school started and another in time for Christmas.

The full catalogs were over a thousand pages, two inches thick, and heavy. We not only ordered clothes, shoes, and underwear from the catalog but also baby chicks. The Sears and Roebuck catalog was much like Lowes, Amazon, and Tractor Supply stores all rolled into one. Montgomery Ward also had a large catalog very similar to Sears and Roebuck.

> *WHITE LEGHORN CHICKS – DAY-OLD*
> *For heavy egg production, our vigorous White Leghorns are bred from proven layers. Small-bodied birds convert feed to eggs economically. Strong, healthy chicks shipped direct from the hatchery in ventilated cartons. Guaranteed live delivery anywhere in the U.S.A.*

The 1950s-style recreated Sears and Roebuck catalog listing for chicks

The catalog also provided us with entertainment. We would lie belly-down on the floor and flip through the pages; wondering who bought such expensive things and where and how they lived. We spent hours looking at and talking about the pictures.

The catalog served as our encyclopedia and definitely provided a good pastime since we had no TV and very few toys to play with while inside the house at night. I think we actually learned a lot about the rest of the world simply by looking at the pictures in the catalog. It also likely improved our reading skills without us knowing or even having to think about it.

Old catalogs weren't discarded; they were given new life and added value by being used to start fires, line cabinet shelves, and provide toilet paper in our outhouse.

The nearest place to buy clothes, including shoes from a retail store, was in Leitchfield or Elizabethtown, about 15 miles away - a long way back then. Therefore, most of our clothes were purchased by mail order through the catalog.

Mom always thought buying things from the catalog was cheaper and easier than making trips to town and buying from physical stores. That would have been right if she hadn't had to send so many things back. Mom spent a lot of money on postage to send items back to exchange them for a different size. She also spent considerable time re-packaging and making trips to the post office to mail them back.

Another reason she may have preferred ordering by mail was that she could order just a few items at a time, and even try to fit one kid at a time, rather than having to have so much money up front.

She also used the Cash-On-Delivery (C.O.D.) approach for paying, which was a common practice back then. C.O.D. allowed us to delay payment until the item was delivered. That worked out well because you weren't having to pay up front and risk not getting your money back if the item was out of stock or if it had been discontinued. The C.O.D. approach allowed us to either pay the mail person for the item or go to the post office and pick it up.

Mom would start ordering shoes and overalls for us soon after school let out for the summer. We didn't need the shoes right away because we went barefoot essentially all the time during the summer.

Since the overalls were also for school, they weren't needed until fall either. But Mom knew that using mail order to get us outfitted for the next school term would be a long process, so she started almost as soon as school let out for the summer.

It seemed she spent the whole summer trying to get the right size shoes and overalls for us three boys. But somehow, she always got it done in time for the start of school in the fall.

She would place an order for the size she thought we needed, and when they arrived, they wouldn't fit, and she would have to send them back and try a different size, usually bigger.

Sending something back and exchanging it was not easy back then without the internet or phones. Order forms and return documents had to be filled out, and the articles had to be taken to the Post Office for return.

We always dreaded it when we finally received a package. More than likely, it was either shoes or overalls for us that had been ordered from the Sears and Roebuck Catalog. After seeing Mom get a package and open it, we could usually begin a reasonably accurate countdown till she would holler at one or all of us to come in and try something on. It was almost like

she thought she'd better make us hurry and try them on because we might grow out of them before nightfall.

We would much rather take a whipping than try on
clothes. But we knew there was no way to get out of it, so we
might as well get it over with. We also knew this was likely not
going to be a one-time and done event.

We were always afraid the new clothes were not going to
fit – and they rarely did. Mom would make us try them on two
or three times before she would give up and finally admit she
was going to have to send them back again and try a different
size.

Often, by the time she received the size she was trying to
get, our feet and bodies had grown, and she would have to start
all over. Sometimes, it seemed she was blaming us for growing
so much over the summer.

I can almost still hear her fussing as she made us try them
on again, just to be sure they wouldn't fit. Sometimes, she
would delay the decision to return them by saying, "Maybe
your feet are swollen, so try them on again in the morning".
That always made us cringe because we dreaded starting the
"trying on ritual" again the next morning, especially since we
knew they still weren't going to fit.

She would swear that next time, she was not going to fool
around with ordering shoes and clothes, and we would have to
go to the store and pick them out. But the next summer, she
would try ordering one more time, and again spend all summer
sending them back and forth. Juanita was much smaller, and
most of her clothes were homemade by Mom or our Grandmother Ma. Our grandmother would hold a newspaper up to
Juanita's chest and mark the position of the holes for the arms

and the neckline. She then laid the newspaper down on the clothing material, cut out the holes, and then sewed the dress, or whatever she was making. Juanita remembers the clothing items always fitting perfectly. She is wearing one of her homemade dresses in the photo of her and her cousin Paul.

Juanita Wearing a Homemade Dress and Cousin Paul Risner

Mom usually tried to buy our clothing a little larger than we needed just so it would take longer for us to outgrow them. At the start of the school year, our clothes would be too big, and by the time school ended for the summer, they were too small. Sometime around midyear, they must have fit us just right.

I hated wearing new overalls for the first time because they were extremely stiff, and it was obvious to everyone they were new. But, after wearing them a few days, and then scrubbing them in the wash tub, they felt and looked just fine.

19

Juggling in the Corn Field

One day my granddaughter was visiting, and three or four tennis balls happened to be lying on a nearby table. Without thinking, I scooped them up and juggled them in the air. She was amazed I could do that and asked, "Granddad, how do you do that, and would you teach me in the same way you learned?"

Her simple question prompted me to laugh out loud and sent me straight back to my childhood. I had to explain that I wasn't laughing at her, but at the thought of me teaching her in the same way I learned to juggle.

I went on to explain that to teach her in the same way, we would first have to buy a horse and then find a plowed field. She would then have to learn to balance and ride standing up on two or three logs tied together as she drove the horse back and forth across the dusty field. That was called dragging the ground to break up larger clods of dirt and provide a smoother planting surface. After she learned that, she would hold the reins to the horse in one hand, and then bend over and grab two or three clods of dirt and begin practicing juggling them using the one free hand.

I also told her that while practicing, it would be really important that she not fall in front of the drag. If she did that, the juggling lessons would almost certainly be over.

I could tell from her facial expression that she probably wouldn't be learning to juggle anytime soon, at least not in the same manner I did.

We usually grew ten to fifteen acres of corn as feed for the animals and to provide enough for us to grind some into corn meal and boil a few ears for dinner. We used all the corn that we grew and never had any left to sell.

We always looked forward to the corn becoming ripe enough to boil on the cob – we called them "roastneers." We also looked forward to fried corn, which was prepared by cutting and scraping it from the cob and frying it in a skillet.

Removing the silks was the hardest part of preparing the corn for boiling or frying. These always seemed to grow down into the ear of corn and tightly between the rows of corn grains. Even after pulling, brushing, and washing, a few silks were left on the ear of corn.

Similar to other crops, growing corn required considerable labor and some luck in getting the right amount of rain. Corn has shallow roots, making it especially sensitive to too little or too much water.

As soon as the ground dried in the spring, we would plow the field using both of our horses and a single turning plow. The turning plow was heavy, weighing around 100 pounds, and had to be dragged around and turned in the opposite direction at the end of each pass. The person doing the plowing had to walk behind the plow while holding it upright and guiding it to keep the furrows at the right width and depth.

The turning plow was too heavy for me, so plowing was left to my Dad and older brother Billy. However, I was able to cultivate tobacco and corn using a smaller cultivating plow. These weren't nearly as heavy as a turning plow, but still required all my strength to control it and pull it around at the end of each row.

Each pass of the turning plow would cut and turn over strips of soil about ten inches to a foot wide and six inches deep. Plowing a relatively small field about 400 feet wide would require over 400 trips with the horses and plow from one end of the field to the other.

It's a good thing we didn't know it back then, but plowing an area of only one acre required walking over eight miles while struggling to control the heavy plow and, at the same time, drive the horses.

Plowing the entire fifteen-acre field required the horses to pull the plow 120 miles. Of course, the person controlling and guiding the plow also had to walk the 120 miles while attempting to keep the plowed furrows at the right depth and width and the plow away from stumps, roots, and big rocks. Quite often, the plow would hang up on something, such as a large root, and the horses couldn't pull it loose. The heavy plow then had to be freed by dragging it backwards - significantly increasing the burden on the person doing the plowing. Both the horses and the person were dead tired by nightfall. Dad would feed the horses well and make sure they were well rested before going at it again about daylight the next morning.

Both hands were needed on the plow handles, so most people doing the plowing either looped or tied the reins from the horses around their backs or shoulders to remain in easy reach. This was a dangerous but necessary practice. Many people were hurt, and even killed, by the horses becoming spooked and entangling the person in the reins.

After the field was plowed, it had to be disked one or two times to break up the large dirt clods. This was physically easier on people doing the disking, as they were able to ride on top of the disk. However, they did eat a lot of dust and were wearing a thick coat of it at day's end.

The plowed field made it much harder for the horses to walk across it while pulling both the disk and the person riding it.

Most of the time, after being disked, the field still needed to be dragged to further smooth the dirt and break up the larger dirt clods before planting. We made our drags by chaining two or three long, heavy poles together and using our horses to drag them across the field.

Standing on the drag and guiding the horses was sort of boring to me. As I explained to my Granddaughter, to pass the time, I would guide the horses with one hand and juggle dirt clods with the other hand. That was probably not the safest way to drag the field, but it worked for me.

When working with horses, there is always the danger that they will become scared, get completely out of control, and maybe even take off running. I only experienced a runaway horse once, but it was a scary event. As she ran, the cultivating plow went with her. It would bounce around and sometimes hit her legs and feet, adding to her panic.

There was always the danger that while running, the horse would get tangled up, fall, and break a leg. Luckily, our horses were never seriously hurt while bolting, nor was the equipment damaged beyond repair. At least once, as shown in the photo, our horse shredded her harness while bolting. About all that was left was the collar. It looks as if she is embarrassed about the whole thing – and she should be.

During prolonged dry spells, the corn would look as if it were completely dried up. But then it would rain, and shortly, the corn was healthy-looking again and growing fast.

In the fall, we would gather the corn by hand, going through the field, row by row, pulling off the ears of corn, and pitching them into piles for pickup later. The dried corn shucks were rough, almost like sandpaper on our hands, wrists, and arms, causing scrapes and bruises that itched, especially at night.

We later used the horses and wagon to pick up all the corn we had piled up. We then used a scoop shovel to unload the corn from the wagon into the corn crib.

Since the corn was stored directly on the floor, it was easy pickings for the mice. They likely took much more than their share.

The corn stalks, left standing after removing the ears of corn, made good feed for the horses and cattle. We used machete-like knives to cut the stalks and then tied them together into shocks using a corn stalk wrapped around the top.

Most of the time, we remembered to wear bandannas around our necks to keep the sharp, dry leaves from cutting and scraping our necks. However, even with the protection, the itching from leaves scraping the neck was awful. Also, one had to slice downward with the sharp knives into the corn stalks to more easily cut the stalks. Since our legs were always near the bottom of the stalk, they were in danger of being accidentally hit with the knife.

Our Horse after Bolting and Tearing up her Harness

One day, while we were cutting corn, Billy did hit his ankle with a corn knife and cut a vein. The blood was spurting out of the wound with each heartbeat. Dad wrapped a handkerchief around his leg, and after a few minutes, the bleeding had stopped, and we got back to work.

The corn shocks were bulky, and we didn't have enough room for them in the barn. We usually just left them in the field until they were needed, then we brought several to the barn at a time.

20

Hog Killing Time

I was around ten years old and had been around cattle all my life, and now I was about to eat beef on a hamburger for the first time.

We always had three or four cows, but their purpose was to produce milk and then, about once a year, have a calf to be sold. I had no idea what happened to a calf once it went to market. I was hoping someone would buy it and turn it loose in a pasture with tall grass. I am not sure if I was even aware that people ate beef.

Our family was on the way to see my grandparents in the mountains near Salyersville and had stopped to visit my Aunt Zelda in Mount Sterling, Kentucky. By the time we got to Mount Sterling, it was past supper time, so Zelda cooked each of us a hamburger, making that occasion not only the first time I had eaten beef, but also the first time I had ever eaten a hamburger.

Meat to me meant hogs, so eating beef was a new and seemingly strange experience for me. I wasn't really sure I even wanted to eat the hamburger. But I was hungry from the long car trip and so ate it anyway. Actually, it wasn't bad, but I declined a second hamburger, saying I was full.

Each year, we fattened one or two hogs to be butchered in the fall, usually around Thanksgiving. We always picked a cool or preferably cold day so the meat would be less likely to spoil.

Hog-killing day was always an exciting time for us. There was a lot of activity, and we mostly just watched the work of handling the heavy hog, but we helped with the lighter jobs.

A fire had to be built, the horse had to be rounded up and harnessed so it could pull the large hog from the hog pen to the butchering area, water for scalding and cleaning had to be drawn from the well, knives had to be found and sharpened, and lots of other preparations had to be completed and ready before the hog was killed.

A key step in butchering hogs was to scald them in hot water, making the hair easier to scrape off. To do that, we would heat the water in a large 50-gallon metal barrel placed over an outside fire. The water had to be hot enough to scald the skin but not so hot as to overheat and partially cook the meat.

As the water heated, Dad would keep checking its temperature by quickly dipping his fingers into the hot water. I am not sure how accurate that was, but it always seemed to work well enough.

After everything was ready, Dad would shoot the hog with our 22 rifle and then immediately cut its throat to allow as much of the blood to drain from the carcass as possible. After the hog was killed, it was dipped into the hot water for just a few seconds and then quickly removed. That was the hardest and most dangerous part of the butchering process, as the hogs were large and heavy, with some weighing up to 400 pounds.

Scalding the larger hogs required at least two strong men holding onto either the hog's front or back legs. The barrel of hot water was slightly tilted to lean against a wagon, and the men were on the bed of the wagon with the hog. Being that high up allowed the men to more easily slide the hog into and out of the water without having to lift the hog's full weight.

Everyone had to be careful to not tip over the barrel, as the scalding water was really hot and could cause serious burns. The barrel would only hold one end of the hog at a time, so one end had to be lowered into the barrel, left there for a few seconds, and then pulled out. The hog was turned around, and then the other end was placed into the barrel in the same manner.

Once scalded, the hair was scraped off with butcher knives - a job we kids helped perform. It usually took at least 30 minutes to scrape all the hair off a large hog.

The hog was then hung upside down, and the intestines and other organs were removed. I still remember the steam coming off the intestines and how bad they smelled as they fell out of the hog carcass and into a wash tub.

The meat was carefully processed to last as long as possible and to be used in different ways. Sometimes, neighbors would help with the butchering and, as a thank-you, would be given some of the tenderloin or bacon.

Tenderloin is the leanest and best-tasting cut of meat, but it is so lean, it doesn't cure or keep well like the hams or bacon. To be sure it didn't spoil, Mom fried it in a skillet right away, and we ate it while the rest of the meat was still being processed.

We usually had to keep chasing our dogs and cats away as they wanted in on the feast.

To preserve the hams, Dad rubbed them with copious amounts of salt to draw out moisture, then hung them up to cure. When fried, the ham was delicious but extremely salty.

Some of the meat contained a lot of fat and was best suited for sausage, so it was cut into strips and ground into sausage using a hand-cranked grinder. Pepper and other seasonings were added in, and then the sausage was stuffed into long cloth sacks, about two inches in diameter, ready for storage and later use.

I still don't like the thought of it, but at least once, part of the hog's intestines were cleaned and used as sausage bags. That was a common practice at that time, but not even close to my preferred storage method.

Some of the sausages were fried and then put into fruit jars and canned for use later in seasoning beans and cabbage. Some of the canned sausages, along with a biscuit, were taken to our one-room school for lunch. The biscuit was cold and the sausage greasy, but I was ready for it when it finally became time to eat.

Part of the hog fat was chopped into small chunks and boiled down into lard to be used as cooking oil. Mom made lard by melting it down in a large black cast-iron kettle over an outside fire. The melted oil and remaining fat pieces were strained, and the pure liquid was put into jars or cans, some as large as 5 gallons. As the liquid fat cooled, it solidified into pure white lard.

Mom also used the cast-iron kettle and some of the fat, along with lye and wood ashes, to make lye soap.

21

Memorable Times

Rural kids didn't need much to find excitement, as the world itself was one big playground. With few toys and plenty of imagination, an ordinary trip to find and bring the cows from the pasture could quickly become a journey through wild Indian country filled with imagined dangers and secret hideouts. A fallen log across a small creek wasn't just a bridge — it was a test of being able to cross a roaring river filled with imaginary dangers below, such as turtles large enough to drag you to their den or lions waiting to gobble you up.

A walking trip to the local grocery might turn into a contest to spot the biggest bird or who could throw a rock and hit a nearby fence post. Even a small patch of woods could hold ever-changing mysteries.

Weather and even work could be the catalyst for adventure. After a summer thunderstorm, we would hurry to the creek to see how high the water had risen, sometimes tossing makeshift boats from bark or sticks into the swiftly flowing waters and wondering how far they would go - maybe the Mississippi River or even the ocean. Winter meant snowball fights and attempts to track a rabbit that had left deep, clear tracks in the snow, all the while pretending it was an outlaw trying to elude capture. Even chores like rounding up and catching chickens became chances to race, compete against each other, or set new limits of endurance. Every day of life was full of simple events that, with a bit of imagination, became lasting adventures.

Imaginations Gone Wild

I was hanging around Dad and a couple of other adults, listening in on their conversations, and trying to pretend I wasn't paying attention. My ears perked up when I heard one of them make a casual comment that a bear had been spotted a couple of weeks earlier. He went on to say it was at least a hundred miles away in an adjacent county.

I had seen pictures of a bear, but that is the closest I had ever been to one. I wasn't even sure bears were real or just beasts of the night that chased me in my dreams.

But that comment captured my attention, and just to be safe, I spread the word to neighboring kids with the warning to watch out. I may have also added a few minor details to what I had heard, such as that the bear was heading our way, stood at least 10 feet tall, and had already eaten several kids.

It didn't take long for the bear alarm to spread among the neighborhood kids. I next heard about it when one kid was swearing on his mother's grave – although she wasn't even dead yet, that he had seen it near their barn and it had twin cubs five feet tall.

We frequently played in the nearby woods, and for a while after that, we talked about the bear and were more or less on guard when we were near the woods.

Days later, Doug and I were playing with our cousins in the woods near a cave and noticed an unfamiliar animal track.

We began wondering if it might be the bear, although none of us had any idea what a bear track looked like.

It wasn't long before we had convinced ourselves it absolutely had to be a bear track, and we had better start keeping an eye out for it. None of us wanted to be the next kid the bear had for lunch.

Shortly thereafter, one of us saw something, which was likely a dark bush or a stump, and started yelling that they could see the bear, and it was coming in our direction and fast.

It didn't take long for all of us to panic and start pushing and shoving each other, trying to be first and highest up a nearby tree. After sitting in the tree for a few minutes, someone mentioned that bears were supposed to be really good at climbing trees. We suddenly realized that by being up in the tree, we were sitting ducks. We decided to get out of there, and quickly.

We jumped out of the tree and took off running as hard as we could for home, a half mile away. Nobody wanted to be the last one in the group, as they would surely be the first one caught and eaten by the bear.

As we ran, we excitedly imagined what the bear would likely do to us, which increased our panic. We were sure it was going to catch and kill us all.

Mom and Dad saw us running toward home and knew something must have happened for us to be so excited. We were completely out of breath and barely able to excitedly swear we had seen the bear. We also claimed it had chased us out of the woods and, for a while, was no more than 10 feet behind us. Actually, in our imagination, it was so close we could hear it growling and gnashing its teeth.

Mom and Dad were inclined not to believe us, but since every one of us was telling the same story, it did cause them some concern. They spent a minute or two looking back toward the woods, just to be sure no bear was chasing us.

After a day or two, we were completely over the fear of the bear and were playing in the woods again as if nothing had happened. But, for a while, Dad did seem a little more careful when near the woods and would look up rather quickly when hearing a tree branch break or a squirrel jumping in the trees.

The Chicken House Hammer

While we lived at our Big Clifty home, I would occasionally walk across the fields to visit with my maternal grandparents. While there, I would usually help out with a few things, such as going over the hill back of the house to the spring and carrying a bucket of water back up the steep hill.

On one occasion, while I was there, my uncles Junior and Ed were replacing the metal roof on their chicken house.

I offered to help them for a few minutes, but then I had to head back home for some reason – maybe to participate in a school play or something similar. Ed was tired and wanted to get a drink of water, so he suggested I take his place on the roof while he was gone. I took his hammer and started driving nails into the new roofing.

Things seemed to be going along pretty well, but then, while trying to start a nail through the metal roofing, the nail slipped, and I hit my thumb with the hammer. That was actually not unusual when trying to start nails in metal roofing.

I dropped the hammer onto the roof and grabbed my thumb. The nail of my thumb was bleeding and immediately started turning black and throbbing like everything. I had forgotten about the hammer, and my foot accidentally hit it. The hammer started sliding toward the edge of the roof. I tried to grab it, but it was too far away.

Ed had just gotten back from getting a drink and was standing where the hammer was about to fall off the roof. I yelled to get his attention, and just as he turned around to see what I wanted, the hammer went over the edge. I didn't see it actually hit him, but it must have been a perfect shot to the top of the head, as I did hear a thud.

The heavy metal hammer almost knocked him to the ground. He had a dazed look on his face as he stumbled to a nearby wagon and sat down. It took him a little while to figure out what had happened to him.

I climbed down from the roof, and we both sat on the wagon nursing our injuries. At first, I was somewhat afraid he would pick up the hammer and hit me with it. But after he saw my thumb, he didn't seem to be blaming me too much for the incident. I reminded him I had to go and left.

I believe I actually got the worst end of the accident because the nail of my thumb hurt like the dickens for a few days, turned black, and eventually came off. Ed had a knot on his head for about a week, and then it went away.

That type of incident is not easily forgotten, and I still remember it well. Neither Ed nor I ever mentioned it again.

The Bee Tree Gets Exciting

One summer, my uncle Earl found a hollow tree that was home to a swarm of bees. He came by our house and asked Dad to help him cut it down and get the honey. They rounded up a two-person crosscut saw, an ax, and a bucket to put the honey in, and headed back to the woods where Earl had seen the tree with a swarm of bees.

My brothers and I went along as we had never seen someone cut a bee tree, and besides, this kind of activity usually turned into an adventure.

They first warned us to stay far back from the falling tree and to watch out for bees, then they moved up close to the tree and began sawing it down using the crosscut saw.

Everything went according to plan until the tree started falling. Then, all of a sudden, Earl threw the saw and started jumping, yelling, and slapping at his legs and crotch area. He then began running in circles while still hitting his crotch. He tripped and fell at least once and almost ran under the slowly falling tree.

Dad didn't know what was wrong or what to do as Earl wouldn't stop running or beating himself long enough to explain or let him help. Dad had been watching the saw and was pretty sure Earl had not somehow been cut with the sharp saw teeth.

My brothers and I started backing up as we thought maybe he had gone mad with rabies or something, and might even pick up the ax and come after us.

Even our dog seemed confused and a little worried, and began barking and keeping a keen eye on Earl as he continued to do what looked like an Indian war dance.

While doing all that jumping, running, and falling, Earl was finally able to get his belt loose and drop his pants. A small ground squirrel took advantage of its freedom opportunity and scampered out of Earl's pants and ran off into the woods - apparently uninjured from all the beating it had just taken.

The little squirrel had been in the hollow tree, but abandoned ship as soon as it sensed the tree begin falling. It apparently mistook Earl's pant leg for another nearby hollow tree and quickly dashed up the inside of his pants legs. Using its sharp claws, the squirrel had no problem quickly climbing Earl's leg all the way up to the crotch area. It hung on tight and moved from front to back as Earl jumped around, beating at it.

Earl had been looking up at the falling tree to make sure it wasn't going to fall on him and hadn't seen the ground squirrel racing toward him, and so had no idea what had gone up the inside of his pants. He knew it was an animal of some kind, or maybe even a snake, and was desperate to get it out of there.

After the excitement and Earl's heart rate had died down enough for him to get his pants back on, they found that the bees had just started building their honeycombs, and so, there was no honey. Earl said he needed to go home and meekly headed off. The rest of us gathered up the tools and also went home.

Earl suffered only a few scratches from the squirrel's claws, and as far as I know, he never found another bee tree, or if he did, he kept that information to himself.

Buried Treasure

As a child living at our Eastview home, I became fascinated with finding and digging up buried treasure. We didn't have a TV, so I didn't get the motivation from that. Possibly, it was from books, or it could have been that I occasionally heard people talking about burying their money in the yard rather than trusting a bank. I would dream of digging up someone's long-lost bankroll and using the money to sail the world and visit far-off places.

I had heard tales from kids I considered credible sources that there was a pot of gold at the end of rainbows. Several times, I looked from different vantage points and tried to pinpoint exactly where rainbows ended. If I could ever do that, then I planned to dig up the gold. I often wondered why there wasn't a crowd of grown-ups rushing toward it to dig up the gold for themselves.

Several times, I considered rounding up all the neighborhood kids and digging it up to surprise our parents with all the gold. One big problem was that the ends of the rainbows were always in a different place, making it hard to decide where to dig. I never questioned how the pot of gold could keep moving and following the rainbows.

But most of my attention was on finding gold old-timers had buried. I used shovels and hoes and dug a lot of holes in suspicious-looking places just in case they held buried treasure. There were many sunken and raised places, especially in the woods, that I reasoned might have been caused by someone burying treasure.

All I ever found were rocks, old rotted-off fence posts, or muddy water. I decided if I wanted to find buried treasure, then I was going to have to bury it myself and dig it up later.

I rounded up about a dollar's worth of coins I found lying around the house, and put them in an old metal coffee can with a little note including the date, which I now believe was 1948. I then found an ideal place to bury it halfway between the back of the chicken house and an apple tree. I only buried it about six inches deep.

I drew a map of where my treasure was buried, planning to use it in about a year to find the treasure. But, true to form, about two days later, I had lost the map, and within another day or two, I was on to some other adventure and had totally forgotten about even burying the treasure.

Shortly thereafter, we sold the Eastview farm and moved to our Big Clifty home. As far as I know, the coins are still where I buried them, 75 years ago. More than likely, both the chicken house and apple tree are long gone. It has been a long time, but every once in a while, I think about that treasure and wonder if I could remember the location well enough to go back there and dig it up. I am almost certain I could find it using a metal detector. The coffee can and note are probably gone, but the coins should still be there unless the spot has been plowed or had concrete poured over it.

Someday, when I am back in the area, I may stop and talk to the current owners and maybe offer to share the treasure with them if they let me hunt for it and dig it up.

Billy Saves Our Watermelons

Watermelon vines took up a lot of space, so we usually planted those completely separate from our garden. We tried planting watermelons in the corn rows, but that never worked out very well. The corn shaded the watermelons, resulting in fewer and smaller melons.

One year, we planted a large watermelon patch of about a quarter-acre in the very back of our field, farthest from our house, and in the very spot another house had once stood years earlier and had now completely vanished.

The only visible trace that the earlier house had even existed was the bountiful yellow buttercup flowers that sprang up each year in late March. They roughly outlined where the yard used to be and seemed to be trying to hold on to the past as a reminder to everyone that other children once played and grew up here.

Most farms had a watermelon patch with the exact location a secret. That was because quite often, just for fun - and to have something to do - boys would get together and try to slip unnoticed into someone's watermelon patch late at night. They would unintentionally destroy many of the melons by plugging them with their pocket knives, attempting to find a couple of really ripe ones to carry back to a favorite hangout. They often smashed three or four others on the ground, and scooped out and ate a handful or two of the ripest ones right there in the patch. Watermelon patches were especially vulnerable on Halloween night.

Neither Billy nor I was completely innocent, and at one time or another, had helped ourselves to a delicious watermelon from a neighbor's patch. I never "borrowed" more than one melon or destroyed any of the others. I suspect the same is true for Billy. We understood how irritating it was to be on the receiving end of a raid that did serious damage to one's watermelon patch. It took a lot of work all summer long to grow big watermelons.

One time, while Billy was hanging out with some of his buddies, they got the idea to raid the watermelon patch of a nearby farmer known for growing lots of big watermelons. They searched for his melon patch for at least an hour, but couldn't find it because of the dark, moonless night.

Everyone was now craving a ripe melon and began wondering how they could get one. Eventually, they got around to asking Billy if they could go to our patch, but only get one or two to eat. They promised to leave the rest alone.

Billy didn't want his buddies to know where our patch was located - he didn't trust them to leave the melons alone once he was not with them. He finally relented but told the group he would go by himself and get one from our patch if they would remain at the road, so no one else would know exactly where the patch was located.

That seemed like a good plan at the time, but it didn't work out the way Billy intended. Just as he feared, a couple of his buddies betrayed him by watching as he went to get the melons, and by doing so, learned the location of our melon patch.

Luckily, one of the guys in the group became Billy's informant. He let him know when the rest of the group planned to take advantage of their newly gained knowledge and raid our melon patch.

On the night of the planned raid, Billy hid near our watermelon patch with a loaded shotgun, determined to protect the watermelons by giving the entire group a good scare.

He could hear them coming through the field, laughing about how they had tricked him into revealing the location of the melon patch. Just as they reached the edge of the patch, Billy jumped up and fired two quick blasts of the shotgun into the air. The sound of those shotgun blasts on that late, clear night, ricocheting back and forth through the nearby woods and hills, made the watermelon patch sound like an active warzone.

Everyone nearly ran over each other getting out of there and were soon gone. Billy had saved the watermelon patch; it was left alone and never bothered again.

Everyone continued as good friends, and all laughed about that failed raid for years afterwards.

Picking Blackberries

One morning, Mom was canning blackberries we had picked a day or so earlier, and asked me to go back to the blackberry patch and pick about another quart. She needed a few more to finish filling a half-gallon jar she had cleaned, thinking she had enough berries left to fill it. I selected a small bucket and headed across the field to a fence row where we had found the other berries.

The fence with the blackberry briars ran along the very edge of a ditch that only held water during heavy rains, but had a steep bank. I had found almost enough berries, but needed a handful or two more to be sure I had enough to fill the jar. I noticed several big black berries on briars at the bottom of the ditch, and close to the bank. I decided that if I could get to those, then I could easily get more than enough berries.

The fence was too close to the ditch for me to climb over, but I noticed a place where I could barely crawl under and then slide down the bank into the ditch. Once in the ditch, I would be hemmed in by the briar patch, but I figured I could reach all the berries I needed and then climb back up the bank, scoot under the fence, and be back out of the ditch. That way, I could get out of the ditch without having to walk barefoot through the briar patch.

I held onto my bucket of berries as I crawled under the fence and started sliding down the bank. When I reached the bottom, I sensed a bunch of flies buzzing around my head. But, I soon realized they weren't flies – they were yellow jacket wasps that had been living in a hole in the bank. They apparently weren't happy I had slid across their nest, and so started dive bombing my neck and bare back.

I had nothing to fight them with, so I started slinging the bucket of berries at them. Yellow jackets and berries were flying everywhere, and I was still getting stung. I threw my now-nearly-empty bucket to the ground and took off running, even though I was barefoot, shirtless, and in the middle of a briar patch, at the bottom of a ditch. Somehow, I made it through the briar patch with only a few thorns in my feet and a few more stings before the yellow jackets gave up chasing me and headed back to their nest in the bank.

I was stung at least ten times, and no way I was going back to retrieve my bucket. It didn't really matter anyway, since the berries I had picked were now scattered all over the ditch.

I went home with no bucket and no berries and looking as if a bear had attacked me. Mom treated my stings with some homemade paste, which helped some. Yellow jacket stings hurt more than any other wasp, and it took forever for the stinging to stop.

I was glad that Mom decided we had enough berries anyway and that we should leave the bucket where I had thrown it until winter, when the yellow jackets would be gone.

I still remember the helpless feeling of being trapped in a ditch, barefoot and no shirt, in the middle of a blackberry patch with yellow jackets buzzing all around and making kamikaze attacks. I did learn that a bucket of berries does not make a good weapon against fast-flying yellow jackets.

Hunting for Ginseng

Ginseng roots have been used for centuries as a traditional medicine and currently sell for up to $125/pound when dried. Ginseng is extremely rare in the wild and is now a protected species in Kentucky and other states.

Ginseng is slow-growing and thrives in woody areas, especially around steep hills and cliffs. Anytime I was in the woods where it might be growing, I would keep one eye out for it. It was fun to hunt for it because it involved a lot of walking, following creeks, and climbing steep forest slopes, which made a perfect outing for young boys.

Usually, a friend and I would search for ginseng in the fall when it was likely to have bright red berries, making it easier to spot. We would only dig the roots of older, mature plants, and when we found plants with small red berries, we would plant the berries nearby, hoping they would sprout and produce more ginseng.

Although we would usually walk for miles, we returned most of the time with empty pockets. That was partly because we did nearly everything except actually hunt for the ginseng. Other temptations, such as looking for squirrel holes and nests in the trees, walking fallen trees, climbing rock ledges, hunting for hazel nuts and persimmon trees, and throwing rocks at leaves and twigs floating down the creek, took up most of our time.

It's interesting that when Kentucky enacted regulations for ginseng harvesting in 1982, they essentially mirrored the practices we had followed as kids back in the 40s and 50s – hunt only in the fall, only dig the roots of mature plants, and

Wild Ginseng - Plant on Top; Roots on Bottom (Plant Photo from USFWS)

plant all ripe seeds nearby. It seems we were doing the right thing without even knowing it.

Due to the plant's scarcity, we were never able to find more than one or two plants at each location. I kept everything I could find and never sold any of it. I kept it, hoping that the next time we went ginseng hunting, we would find a large patch and I would have a bigger payday. It seems that never happened. I still have about three ounces of ginseng roots, which is the total of all I found as a youngster.

I suspect that by now they are too dry. It doesn't matter, as I will never sell them, because they are a physical reminder of the good times my friends and I had, over 75 years ago, searching for them as we walked through the woods, climbing and falling up and down the hills. While hunting for it, we would laugh at how close we came to falling in the creek and how one of us fell into a hole and had to be pulled out. During those trips, we would challenge each other to see who could climb the highest on a large grape vine or be the first to climb a small tree and hang on as the top bent over toward the ground.

I also remember our excitement when we would spot a small clump of the ginseng berries and how we would carefully dig out the roots to avoid breaking them or disturbing a nearby younger plant.

22

What Time Is It?

For all the years we lived in Big Clifty, it seemed as if no one ever really knew for sure what time it was or exactly when they were supposed to be somewhere.

Meeting Creek bordered our farm and was the boundary between Eastern and Central Time Zones. In addition, the creek served as the border between Hardin and Grayson Counties. Our house and farm were in the Eastern Time Zone on the Hardin County side of the creek. However, our address was Big Clifty, which is on the other side of the creek and thus in Grayson County.

We usually went through Big Clifty, about three miles away, to get just about anywhere. As soon as we crossed the small bridge spanning the creek, we would leave Hardin County and immediately enter Grayson County. After reaching Big Clifty, if we turned right on Highway 62 toward Leitchfield, we would remain in Grayson County and the Central Time Zone. However, if we turned left on Highway 62 toward Elizabethtown, we soon reentered Hardin County and the Eastern Time Zone.

Things got really complicated and confusing twice a year during the national switch between Daylight Saving Time and Standard Time. Many of our neighbors had a habit of calling

Daylight Saving Time "Fast Time". Other residents would call the Eastern Time Zone "Fast Time." That really added to the confusion. When people said something like "I will be there at 5 o'clock fast-time", most people had no idea what they really meant.

To help keep things straight, most everyone eventually got into the habit of specifying which time they meant by adding a location identifier. If they were going to come over at 5 o'clock, the most meaningful thing to say was "I will be there at 5 o'clock Leitchfield time". If they said that, then you could figure out what time they were actually planning to come over. If they didn't specify a location when talking about time, then the only way to know for sure was to ask and then take your best shot at what they really meant.

No one came up with a good solution, and the issue is probably still causing missed appointments and friendly arguments.

23

Long-handled Underwear

It would not have been easy to endure the cold weather without our long-handled underwear. Made of cotton and covering our whole bodies except head, hands, and feet, they were warm and served as our pajamas. A buttoned trap door was in the back for using the toilet.

Since they were fairly tight-fitting, we soon grew out of them and passed them down from older brother Billy to me, then on to Doug. That meant Billy was usually getting the new pairs, leaving Doug at the end of the line with mostly worn-out pairs. Hand-me-downs were the only way Mom could afford to keep the three of us fast-growing boys in clothes.

During the winter, we wore the long-handles 24 hours/day and only took them off when Mom could no longer stand the smell and insisted we take them off so she could wash them. By then, they could probably stand in a corner themselves.

Juanita was not outside much during the winter and so didn't need to wear long-handled underwear.

Our wood cook stove in the kitchen got more use than any other equipment or tool we had. Not only was it used for cooking, but also for canning vegetables and fruits, and to heat water for washing and bathing. The cook stove had a firebox, an oven, and two or three places for skillets and pots on top.

The fire was kept burning almost continuously to avoid having to rebuild it each time we needed to heat or cook something.

Cooking on top of the stove was fairly straightforward. It was easy to see what was happening to the food item and move it closer or farther from the firebox to adjust the cooking temperature.

Back then, the oven temperature could not be determined accurately. One just built the fire in the firebox, and when the oven felt hot, by sticking a hand inside, whatever was being baked would be placed into the oven. Most recipes used "cook until done" rather than giving time and temperature. Most stoves didn't have a glass front and were opened several times to check how well the item was cooking.

During the winter, it was good to have the extra heat from the cook stove. However, during summer months, the fire, which was needed to can beans, tomatoes, and other garden vegetables or fruit, heated the entire house to an almost unbearable condition. I have no idea how Mom was able to stand the heat while canning during the sweltering summer days of August. She would spend the entire day in the cramped kitchen with a fire and pressure cookers, without air conditioning or even fans.

Since the kitchen stove was used so much, we had to cut and split wood for it year-round. It required a lot of manual wood splitting with an ax to feed the small firebox.

Splitting wood with an axe is dangerous, but we were taught early on to keep feet and legs out of the way of the axe. Still, accidents could easily happen, such as the axe head coming off, the handle breaking, or the axe taking an errant bounce

- all of which could seriously hurt the person splitting the wood.

For some reason, we called wood for the kitchen stove "stove wood" and wood for the living room stove "firewood." I don't know if that was a widely accepted distinction in the purpose of the wood or if that was just our way of keeping track of which type of wood we were talking about.

Our wood pile – where we cut and stacked our wood – was near the barn, about 200 feet from the house. We kept some of both types of wood stacked on the back porch for use at night and during rain or snowstorms. Nothing was worse than having to get up in the middle of the night and go all the way to the barn in deep snow or hard rain to get more wood.

Getting the wood while it was snowing or when snow was on the ground was actually easier than when it was raining. The snow helped with natural lighting, but when it was raining, one first had to locate and light a lantern. Then the lantern had to be carried along with the wood, and at the same time, try to keep a cover over the head.

Having to get up on a cold, rainy night and go to the woodpile tended to motivate us to bring in the wood while it was still daylight and, for sure, before going to bed.

Our stove, used for heating our home, was always near a corner of the living room so the stove pipes could be near the chimney without being in the way. During the winter, we tried to keep a fire going all night by putting a large chunk of wood in the stove just before going to bed. However, it usually burned up in the middle of the night, and the house then got colder fast. Most of the time, there would still be a few hot coals under the ashes, making it easier to restart the fire the next morning.

After the fire went out, we were thankful for our long-handled underwear and the pile of quilts Mom had put over us. Mom or Dad was always first to get up, and had a roaring fire by the time the rest of us got up. As soon as our feet landed on the cold floor, we would make a mad dash for the stove.

Mom and Dad's coffee pot was usually left sitting on whichever stove was being used the most. During the winter, that was likely the living room stove. However, in summer, it was usually the kitchen stove. The coffee pot was refilled with water and additional coffee added every day or two, but the old coffee grounds were not emptied except maybe once a week.

I was too young to drink coffee, but I heard a lot of talk about how strong it was. After the pot had been on the stove, without emptying the coffee grounds, for a whole week, the coffee was likely more of a gel than a liquid.

That must be why Mom and Dad would bring a small jar of instant coffee with them when they later came to visit us in Tennessee. After tasting my coffee, Dad would ask if I had forgotten to put the coffee in the pot. He would then add at least three or four spoons of the instant coffee to the coffee we had made.

24

Mom's Medical Practices

Mom's medical practices often worked miracles and fast. If we were thinking we might be too sick to go to school, all Mom would have to do was mention one of her remedies, such as castor oil. Then, all of a sudden, we would decide maybe we were well enough to get out of bed and get ready for school after all.

During the 1940s, doctors routinely made house calls and brought along their medical bag that included simple diagnostic equipment such as a thermometer, stethoscope, and a blood pressure cuff. In addition, the bag would contain several medicines, such as morphine, aspirin, castor oil, and cough syrups.

Calling or sending for the doctor back then was a big deal since most rural people didn't have telephones. Just locating a telephone was hard enough. Then, after finding one, we weren't used to using it, nor did we know the Doctor's phone number. Most of the time, someone drove all the way to E-town to notify the doctor. Needless to say, all that took considerable time.

Since calling the doctor was often considered a last resort, Mom had many opportunities to practice and hone her medical skills. My siblings and I were often sick with colds, fevers, infections, sore throats, and coughs. We also were frequently getting hurt, including having bicycle wrecks, stepping on nails while barefoot, and having a cat or dog bite us. Mom would treat these types of illnesses and injuries, and only have us see the doctor for major issues such as broken bones.

A few of the home remedies Mom used were quite common for the times and very memorable. Vicks Salve was liberally rubbed on the chest and nose for colds. The strong smell of all that Vicks Salve did open our sinuses and let us breathe a little easier, but I am not sure how it was supposed to help the congested chest. Maybe inhaling all those vapors was helpful.

A side benefit of the Vicks Salve was that it was said to keep mosquitoes away. I don't doubt that, but we mostly had our colds in the winter, when mosquitoes were gone anyway.

Mom gave us so much castor oil, I believe she must have thought a spoonful would work miracles and cure anything. Castor oil tasted awful, and too much of it would give you diarrhea. Just the possibility or threat of having to take castor oil stopped us from faking that we were too sick to go to school or to hoe tobacco that day.

I believe I still occasionally smell some of the Vicks Salve and now and then have a slight taste of castor oil in my mouth. Maybe it permeated my bones, and some of it is still in there.

I am not sure whether some other treatments added value or, in fact, caused harm. For some reason, when we were really sick and coughing a lot, Mom would give us a spoonful of sugar mixed with kerosene. I don't know whether the sugar or the kerosene was supposed to be the active ingredient. I suspect it was the kerosene, and the sugar was added to offset the kerosene taste. If so, the sugar didn't help much, as the combo didn't taste much better than drinking pure kerosene.

I remember it left a terrible taste in our mouths, and sometimes it would burn a sore throat. The taste and burning took a long time to go away. Since we were around the open flames in the stoves and lamps, it is a wonder we didn't catch on fire after her kerosene treatments.

I don't recall if it actually helped our coughs or just motivated us to steer clear of Mom when we needed to cough.

We seldom complained about being sick because the cure was usually worse for us than the illness. However, most of the time, Mom would notice that we had a fever or weren't eating as usual and begin treatments. After administering a dose of kerosene, she often asked, "Are you feeling better?" – the answer was always "much better."

For poison ivy rashes, my Grandmother would partially burn old rags and rub the soot on the rashes to reduce the itching. That may have actually helped by keeping us from scratching the area so much. She also claimed warts could be removed by rubbing them with a piece of raw meat and then placing the meat beneath the steps of the house. I have no idea how that was supposed to remove warts or how she came up with that particular medical practice.

Most of the time, if a remedy such as the one for wart removal didn't work, it was the patient's fault for not doing exactly what they were supposed to do.

Some remedies she administered didn't seem to work, but at least made you temporarily feel better, such as eating honey or gargling salt water for a sore throat and taking a teaspoon of sugar and whiskey for coughs. Dad frequently had heartburn and would drink a large glass of water with a spoonful of baking soda in it.

I often had the hiccups as a child, and none of the so-called "proven cures" worked to stop them. I drank glasses full of water, stood on my head, jumped up and down, and held my breath until blue in the face. Another accepted practice was to scare them away, and the whole family seemed to delight in administering that particular cure. I don't know if it worked or not, but having the life scared out of you constricted the throat, temporarily slowing the hiccups.

We gave Mom plenty of reason to worry about us being sick or hurt. I began early, developing pneumonia when I was two years old, and according to Mom, I was sent home from the hospital to die. It must have been pretty bad because even now, if I go to a new doctor, I have to explain scars on my lungs.

Around the sixth grade, I developed Bright's disease, which was a kidney ailment that caused serious swelling of my face, giving Mom at least three months of almost constant worry.

Billy's legs were run over by the dual back wheels of a school bus, and he fell out of the back of a truck and broke his arm.

Doug loved to climb and broke his arms several times, falling out of trees and barn lofts. That shouldn't be surprising, seeing the photo of him standing on top of the basketball goal when he was definitely old enough to know better. He also stepped on rusty nails much more often than either Billy or me.

When she was very young, Juanita's hip hurt as she walked. Several people would tell Mom it was probably just a put-on to get carried, but Mom knew better. She would often carry her even when she was three or four years old. Juanita has since had at least two operations on her hip to correct issues that started when she first began walking.

As soon as the weather turned a little warm in May, we would start begging Mom to let us go barefoot, lying to her that the ground was hot. She would finally give in, and then within a couple of days, we were all sick, just as she knew we would be. She would pull out the Vicks Salve, and each night at bedtime, the entire house had the recognizable Vicks Salve smell.

By the end of summer, our feet were probably as tough as shoe leather.

When I was around ten years old, for some still unknown reason, I developed large blisters on my shoulder. They were at least an inch in diameter with severe redness over the entire area. We were always getting strange bumps and bruises, so Mom wouldn't have given it a second thought, except a salesman, selling cleaning supplies such as brooms and mops, happened to stop by and noticed my blisters.

He didn't help much by telling Mom that he had seen a kid a few months before that had blisters just like mine, and two days later, he was dead. That unsolicited assessment of my potential demise sent Mom straight into a panic mode. It actually didn't bother me because my cousin and I were planning to go fishing the next day, and the Salesman's two-day life projection would still allow me to go.

Doug Standing on Top of a Rickety Basketball Goal

Mom wanted to send for the doctor immediately, but Dad finally calmed her down and used a needle to puncture and drain each of the blisters. He assured her that we would call the doctor early the next day if they weren't healing. I believe Mom stayed up, or at least awake all night, while I slept soundly.

As Dad suspected, the next morning, the blisters and the redness had almost disappeared, and the panic alarm was shut down. I don't remember for sure, but I suspect the salesman didn't sell anything to Mom that day.

We never saw a dentist unless we needed a back tooth pulled. We pulled front teeth and others that were loose, using strings or pliers. I had many a tooth removed, almost painlessly, by tying a string between the tooth and a doorknob and then slamming the door.

We occasionally brushed our teeth, and when we did, we used baking soda. I don't recall any of our family ever having fillings or teeth professionally cleaned. For toothaches, we would place chewing tobacco or hold a small rag soaked in whiskey on the ailing tooth. If that didn't work, we tried pulling it.

We went barefoot all summer long and were often playing or working in the barn, where there were lots of opportunities to step on rusty nails. Mom would worry that one of us would get tetanus - we called it lockjaw - from stepping on the nails, getting splinters in our feet and hands, and being bitten by dogs or cats. Tetanus vaccines were available during the 1940s and '50s, but not yet routinely given at school, especially in rural areas such as ours.

After stepping on a nail, about all Mom could do for it, if we even told her about the nail, was wash it really well and pour alcohol on the wound. If we didn't have alcohol, she would use kerosene. The stinging from the alcohol or kerosene made us forget about the pain from the nail puncture, and we were soon back playing in the same place. More than likely, the board and nail were still lying where we stepped on them, awaiting another victim. We began getting vaccines at school during the mid-1950s. We always hated it when a nurse would show up at school to give shots. We usually knew when she was coming, but couldn't get out of it because a note had been sent home to our parents advising them to be sure we came to school that day.

As I recall, refusing to take the shots was not an option. Besides, our parents would always worry about us getting diseases and were glad to see us get the shots.

I believe standing in line to get the shots was actually worse than receiving the shot itself. As we moved forward in the line, I would try to act brave, as if I didn't mind getting the shot. I would almost pass out from worrying that I might pass out in front of my friends. It didn't help much when a kid in front of you would start crying and resisting the shot.

We occasionally had ring-shaped, red, and itchy spots on our bodies that most people called ringworm. Mom may have thought they were real worms, but they were actually a fungal infection common in rural kids in the 1940s. Once, Mom decided we might have worms, and gave us all doses of a worm medicine that was commonly available during the 1940s. Even if we didn't have worms, the medicine was likely beneficial, as it would remove all types of parasites from the body.

A few times, Mom would hear that someone in our school had head lice. That would prompt her to give each of us a close inspection and then occasionally administer a treatment, just in case. That must have worked, because I don't remember any of us ever actually having head lice.

Since we went barefoot all summer, it was inevitable that one of us would soon get a major bruising or pain in the foot and hobble to Mom. Our problem may have been due to a cow stepping on our foot, dropping a heavy rock or block of wood on our toe, or simply striking our toes on a rock while running.

Mom would first check to see that our foot or toe didn't seem broken. She would then prepare a pan of hot water with Epsom salts and have us soak our feet. That did seem to help.

One of Mom's biggest worries when we were young was that we might get polio. She was especially worried when we had a fever and were aching all over. Her concern was heightened by seeing pictures of people with polio in "iron lungs". The development of the polio vaccines lifted a major burden from her shoulders, and she was adamant about us getting the vaccine.

Medical practices, both at the professional level and in the home, have undergone significant change since the 40's. Those changes, coupled with major lifestyle changes, have steadily increased the U.S. average life expectancy from 62 in 1940 to 79 in 2024.

The advent of health insurance, including Medicare, has encouraged more people to take preventive actions, such as taking medicines to lower cholesterol and blood pressure levels. Insurance has also led many people to seek medical help for health issues sooner than they may have before they had insurance.

New imaging techniques, such as PET scans, X-rays, MRIs, and CT Scans, have allowed doctors to diagnose and treat illnesses much more quickly and effectively. However, to use them, the patient had to travel to the doctor's office or a lab. By the early 60's, house calls were essentially a thing of the past.

25

Fun and Games

I now occasionally hear young children tell their parents they are bored and ask what they could do for fun. Back then, we never became bored, but if we did, we certainly wouldn't have mentioned to our parents or asked them what we could play or do. We knew what they would likely say, "The hoe is leaning against the fence. Get it and chop some weeds." They would probably be joking, but we weren't going to risk it. It was up to us to decide what to play; then make any needed toys.

We also never expected them to join in when we were playing. If they happened to get a short break from work, they would take the opportunity to sit down and rest for a few minutes. Playing a game with the kids, such as hide-and-seek, was not likely on their list of things to do, ever. But at night, Mom might show us how to use the scissors to cut items from folded paper, such as animal faces and fake beards. Dad would challenge us to a game of checkers or show us, for instance, how he used to make whistles from elderberry stalks.

Now, as a parent, grandparent, and even great-grandparent, I have much more time available than my parents did, and I look forward to playing with the grandkids. We make sure we have a variety of toys for us and them to play with when they visit. No doubt they think of us as playmates rather than grand-parents.

Many of today's toys, such as electronic games and re-motely controlled drones, are complex and provide children with learning experiences as they play with them. The toys we made were simple, and the learning experience usually oc-curred while we were making toys rather than while using them. When using a pocket knife to carve a whistle or a sling-shot, we soon learned, through experience, to push the knife away from us and not pull it towards us. We also learned about the different types of wood - which ones would easily carve or split the easiest, which ones would make strong wheelbarrows, or be best for lightweight sleds.

Time passed much more slowly for kids, so we had plenty of time to brag about our recent feats, solve world prob-lems, or talk about how, next week, we might build a boat and float down the creek.

I used to think that life would be so great if we didn't have a tobacco patch to work in or cows to milk. We would then be able to roam and explore all day long without having to pull tobacco worms off the tobacco or chop down the fast-growing weeds. We would have a lot more time to go swimming and fishing, and wouldn't have to hurry home to milk the cows be-fore dark.

I didn't fully realize it at the time, but without tobacco and cows, we would likely be going without clothes and food.

Even though it seemed to us that we were spending too much time helping with all the farm work and other tasks, we still had time to be kids and get plenty of play and exploring time, probably more than we should have.

When not working, we were free to explore or hang around with our siblings or friends. Play time was our time, and we could use it as we wanted as long as we were reasonable and didn't get hurt. We would make and play with our toys such as bows and arrows, popguns, whistles, swings, seesaws, slingshots, and stilts.

With those toys, we could be an army conquering new lands or hunters stalking big game, such as antelope, and bringing home the meat to feed the family and prevent starvation. The stilts and seesaws allowed us to be part of a circus act, and we would bow to the standing ovations. We used the whistles to warn of imminent danger.

In the 1940s, little girls, including Juanita, often made mud pies as one of their favorite cooking creations. With plenty of imagination and no shortage of dirt, they would scoop plain old dirt into pans, jars, or discarded tin plates and add water from a nearby rain barrel or even carry it from the pond. They would pat and shape it until it looked just right and then decorate it with dandelions, pebbles, or bits of grass.

They would then serve their pies to siblings, their rag dolls, or unsuspecting parents, who would take an imaginary bite and acclaim how good they were.

It was a game that cost nothing, required no store-bought toys, and gave a sense of accomplishment, all while letting little girls attempt to copy the cooking they saw their mothers do every day in real kitchens.

As with the mud pies, most things we enjoyed doing cost nothing. I do, however, get the shivers thinking about some of the things we did that were truly unsafe. It seems we were always trying to see who could jump over the highest object, swing the highest on a grape vine, walk the most dangerous log, jump from the highest barn loft or tree, and run the fastest.

Although I always had cuts and bruises, I never got hurt badly enough to call or be taken to the doctor. It was Billy and Doug who occasionally ended up with broken bones.

I do still have a scar on my hip from the time a tree limb I was climbing broke, causing me to fall backwards onto a small glass bottle I was carrying in my back pocket. The cut bled quite a bit, but healed on its own. I also occasionally stepped on old rusty nails and dropped heavy objects on my bare toes.

Our fun included just fooling around in the woods, being near a creek, and playing with toys we mostly made ourselves. We seldom played alone. We always had nearby cousins, friends, or siblings to help decide what to do next and to share the fun with.

Sometimes, our fun could be more like work than play. Some toys, such as stilts, took a long time to make. We had to first hunt for an axe, walk at least a mile searching for tree limbs of the right size and shape, and then take the limbs home and make the stilts.

We often learned the hard way what to do and not do. For a long time, when in the woods, we would find grape vines and swing on them without worrying that they might break and drop us onto rocks or into deep water. Most of the time, we wouldn't even test the vine's strength by pulling on it, but we soon learned that it might be a good idea to do that.

Pretending

We didn't have many manufactured toys, so much of our play involved using our imaginations. When very young, we would pretend that a stick or a broom was a horse and ride it as we romped or raced around the house or yard, yelling "Giddy-up".

Sometimes we would get into an old car and pretend we were going to town or to visit a friend. We would play-drive the car by turning the steering wheel, making motor sounds, and shifting gears to make it up a hill. We would blow the horn to warn people and cows to get out of the way. We would have make-believe crashes and all of us in the car would go flying out and pretend we were hurt or killed.

We were knights and used sticks and paper tubes as swords to drive the enemy from our kingdom.

Marbles

Many adults considered marbles games as gambling; Just about every time they saw us playing marbles, they would caution us, "No playing for keeps."

Our marble games were always played inside the house because that was the only smooth surface we could find. The porch floors were wood with cracks so large our marbles would fall through, and the yard had just enough grass to block our marble games.

We carried the few marbles we had around in our pockets and lost most of them, usually while swinging upside down on a tree limb. We seldom had enough left for a real marble game.

Doug Pretending to Drive; Cousin Ray; Juanita; Cousin Phillis

Mumblety Peg

All the boys I knew carried a pocket knife beginning around 8 years old. They were essential for many work tasks and for making toys. We used them to cut the tops off tobacco, cut string, punch holes, cut holes in boxes, sharpen sticks, play games, and sometimes even to dig into the ground. Most of the time, they weren't very sharp, or if they were, they didn't stay that way for long. After a few finger cuts, we quickly learned how to use them safely.

Mom would often give us knives as Christmas presents because we were always losing them by leaving them lying on the bank of a creek or having them fall through holes in our pockets. Knives also made excellent trading items.

Our knives were required in playing the game Mumblety Peg. To play this game, we put the tip of the knife blade on a body part, such as a fingertip, and while holding it about a foot above the ground, we gave the knife a flip, trying to get it to land blade-first and stick into the ground.

If successful, the other player had to try the same trick. If both succeeded, then the game continued using a different part of the body, such as an elbow, as the base for the blade tip. This continued until one of the players failed to get the knife to stick after flipping it.

Jacks

Young girls, including Juanita, enjoyed playing jacks. It was a simple but exciting game that required good hand-eye coordination, making it fun and challenging.

The game was played by scattering several easily picked up items, called jacks, on the floor or ground, and bouncing a small ball into the air. The idea of the game was to pick up as many of the jacks as you could and catch the ball before it fell back to the floor. Your turn was over when you missed the ball.

Boys also sometimes played jacks, but most of the time they preferred other games.

Hide and Seek

If there were as many as three or four of us playing together, we almost always got around to playing Hide and Seek. One person, selected as "It," would cover their eyes and count to 100 while the rest of us would run and hide nearby. The "It" person would then try to discover where the others were hiding.

When someone was found, they would try to reach the base without having been tagged by the "It" person. Whoever was tagged first became the "It" for the next round.

It usually didn't take long before someone covering their eyes was accused of cheating by either counting too fast or opening their eyes to see where the others were hiding.

Catching Lightning Bugs

There were lots of lightning bugs, especially right after dark and following a slight shower. We would chase them while trying to see who could catch the most. We would have to guess where they would be between flashes; their paths were often random rather than a straight line.

We would make a toy lantern by catching a few lightning bugs, dropping them into a glass jar, and then putting a lid on it. We would punch holes in the lid so they would live at least overnight, and then we would release them unless, as often happened, we forgot all about them.

A few of the lightning bugs suffered a much worse fate, as we would sometimes pinch off their light and stick it on our foreheads as our personal headlights.

Old Maid Card Game

I believe the Old Maid card game was the most exciting and stressful game we ever played as kids. I don't know if kids still play that game or even know what it is.

The deck of Old Maid cards includes two of each card plus one card called the Old Maid.

The rules of the game were quite simple. All the cards were dealt out, and each player would discard any that matched and then form the remaining cards in their hand into a fan shape. The players would then take turns drawing cards from the player on their left. If the drawn card matches one in your hand, you would lay those down and draw again when it was your turn. If you could lay down all your cards, then you were safe and could watch as the other players continued the game. The game loser was the person left with the Old Maid after everyone else had matched and laid down all their cards.

The stressful part of the game was when you were ready to draw a card from the other person's hand. They might have the Old Maid card, and you certainly didn't want that card because, without a matching card, you could be stuck with it. If you got the Old Maid card, you would try to show no emotion so no one would guess you had drawn it. You would also try to position it in your hand so a player would be more likely to select it when drawing a card.

Usually, it was pretty easy to tell when someone drew the Old Maid. The facial expression of the person who drew it would give them away, no matter how hard they tried to hide the fact that they had drawn it. Also, the person who just had the Old Maid drawn from their hand was so relieved they couldn't resist jumping up and down or hollering.

Flower Fights

Blue Vetch is a ground cover with small, blue flowers that have a hook on the stem near the flowers. When we ran across this plant, we couldn't resist challenging each other to a flower fight.

Each of us would pick what we considered to be a strong, healthy flower. We would then connect the heads of the flowers and give a quick snap. The head of the weaker flower would break off, leaving the other one as king.

The loser would look for another strong flower and again challenge the King. Usually, the king would become weaker after a few snaps and lose to a new king.

The fights would continue until we were tired of them and moved on to something else.

Jar Flies

One species of cicada that appears annually is called Jar Flies. These cicadas are large (approximately two inches long) and make a loud buzzing noise by vibrating their wings.

We would catch a Jar Fly, tie a lightweight sewing thread to one of its legs, and then hold on to the string as it flew around us.

It usually didn't take long for the string to come untied or the leg to pull loose from the Jar Fly. Either way, the Jar Fly would fly away and hopefully live a long life.

June Bugs usually appeared around the time blackberries became ripe. They were strong flyers and had large legs, so we would also tie strings to their legs and fly them, much as we did the Jar Flies.

String Buzzer

We could always find uses for strings of any type. One of the things we did with them was to make what we called a string buzzer. We would find or make a small, thin oblong board about six to ten inches long and put a hole through it near one end. Next, we tied a four to six-foot-long string through the hole. We then used the string to swing the board in circles above our heads as fast as we could. The result was a loud buzzing noise.

We would keep swinging the boards until we were tired of that game or one of us had gotten hurt. Most of our injuries were caused by the string coming untied from the board or breaking. Either way, the board would fly outward at high speed and more than once hit another player.

If we weren't paying attention and didn't keep the board in a nearly perfect circle, it would sometimes hit us in the back of the head. That tended to hurt and usually ended the game.

Badminton Equivalent

Most of the time, we used whatever we could find, as a substitute, rather than making a toy. We didn't know what Badminton was, but we sometimes played a similar game, but without real rackets, a net, or a shuttle cock. Instead, we used what we had, which were large metal lard can lids as rackets and a small rock, or sometimes part of an old corncob, for the shuttle cock. We had no trouble knowing when we hit the rock or the cob, because it sounded like a large firecracker going off.

We didn't keep score as it wasn't a competition. The point of the game was to see how long we could keep hitting the rock back and forth with the lids before one of us missed and let it hit the ground.

The good thing about that game was that we could also play it alone. We would try to hit the corncob or rock straight up in the air, and then run beneath it as it fell so we could hit it again.

That usually made for a strange game from an observer's perspective, as it involved a lot of loud noise from the lid hitting the rock and erratic running all over the yard. Since the player was usually looking up while running and trying to see the rock, there was a lot of tripping over objects on the ground and smashing into trees and buildings.

If we were playing near dark, bats would show up and dart after the rock or corncob. After tiring of the Badminton game, we would throw corncobs high into the air and watch the bats turn and swoop towards them until they realized the corn-cobs were not a bug or something edible.

Basketball

Basketball was one of our favorite pastimes. A hoop was nailed to the end of the barn; most of the time, without a net, or else with a net so frayed, the basketball would come out the side of the net instead of the bottom.

The hoop at one time had been round, but after a lot of use and abuse, it was more of an oval than a circle. We usually had a basketball, but it very seldom would hold air and was flat or nearly so. Since it was under-inflated, the basketball wouldn't bounce well enough for us to dribble it. But that was ok, because it was much easier to hold onto it without air in it.

If we didn't have a basketball, we would make do with an old baseball or anything else that was sort of round and not so heavy that it could hurt us.

Our basketball games involved a lot of pushing, shoving, and holding, but they at least gave us plenty of exercise.

Swimming

The creek at our Eastview home was about two miles away, but not too far for us boys. By the time we got there, we were hot and anxious to jump in and cool off. Most of the creek, except for a place or two, was normally too low for swimming, so we just splashed and lay around in the cool water.

One place, near the waterfalls, was deep enough for us to swim a few feet. The falls were 20 feet tall with water shooting over a small cliff into the creek, creating a continuous loud splashing noise and punching out a deep hole at the very base of the falls.

We fished and swam in the pool, and explored the slick rocks behind the stream of water coming over the falls. Sometimes, we stood directly under the falls and let the cold water pound off the mud and whatever else we had accumulated on our bodies.

We would occasionally walk, ride horses, or use our bicycles and go to another small creek with a swimming hole called the "Frog Pond," also about two or three miles from our house.

The Frog Pond was a deep pool, with the water at least six feet deep in some places. It was kept full of water and extremely cold by two water springs flowing out of the side of the hill about 200 feet away. We wondered why it didn't freeze even on the hottest of summer days.

Solid rock, about four feet above the water level, partially surrounded the pool, making an ideal diving platform – actually, our dives were really feet-first jumps.

We always dreaded the initial jump and usually dared each other to be first. In just about all other instances, we would be scrambling to be first, but not at the Frog Pond.

After a short time, we would get up the courage and jump in completely naked. It is a wonder that the shock of the cold water didn't send us straight to the bottom. It felt like jumping into a barrel of ice water.

Sometimes, we would have a countdown from three to zero with the idea that we would jump at the same time. Of course, one of us wouldn't jump at the end of the countdown, making the other mad. But as we acclimated to the cold water, the anger subsided, and we dog paddled as long as we could before having to climb out and warm up.

The Frog Pond had lots of small minnows that would nip at the hairs of our legs almost as soon as we dived in. They didn't hurt, but were very annoying, especially when we stopped moving.

As soon as we were out of the water, we would agree we were never coming back there again -the water was just too cold.

But days later, after working in the tobacco patch all day and being really hot and sweaty, we would decide that the cold water of the Frog Pond would sure feel good and head for it. We would be even hotter by the time we got there, which added to the shock of the cold water. As before, that was going to be our last time swimming in the Frog Pond.

Fishing

We often fished the creek near home, even though we seldom caught anything worth keeping. We dug and used earthworms as bait and cut long, lightweight bamboo stalks for use as fishing poles.

Most of our fishing involved getting lots of nibbles from fish too small to catch and having to keep adding bait. We also spent a lot of time trying to get our fishing lines untangled from the overhanging tree limbs.

We would eventually catch two or three small sunfish, maybe three or four inches long, and take them home, thinking Mom would be excited to clean and cook them.

However, on the way home, we usually found something interesting to do and lay the fish down in the hot sun until we were ready to proceed. By the time we got home, the fish were essentially cooked by the sun and had shriveled up to about one half their original size.

We would give them to Mom to cook, but for some reason, I don't remember ever eating them or what happened to them. I now suspect the hogs enjoyed a small morsel of fish each time we brought them home.

Rolling Tires

I don't know why we did it, but we would often roll and chase after an old tire when we were walking somewhere. I guess it gave us something to do and helped pass the time. In some ways, rolling the tires resembled another practice of ours; kicking tin cans in front of us as we walked.

Just about every time we went across the field to our cousins' house, the tires went along. On the way, we would wind up racing each other, and by the time we got there, we would be covered with sweat and almost too tired from chasing the tires to play

If a tire was big enough, or almost big enough, one of us would try to curl up inside the tire and have someone else roll us. Most of the time, that didn't end well because the one rolling the tire would either go too fast, let it fall over, or purposely try to roll it down a hill. Either way, the one curled up inside the tire usually wound up with several bruises or small cuts.

When we were ready to go back home, we would retrieve our tires and head home, rolling and chasing after them.

We occasionally would ride horses to the creek to go swimming or just for fun. We always rode bareback because we never owned a saddle. Our horses were workhorses and were used to walking, not running. Getting them to even trot was a chore, and we would usually have to resort to a switch. We seldom rode as fast as a gallop, and when we did, it was for a very short distance. Falling off, which we often did while riding at a gallop, always hurt.

Dad bought a mare horse that had been branded, and sometime in her background, she must have been used in roping calves at rodeos, or maybe had worked on a cattle ranch.

The first time Billy rode her, we found out she was different from the farm work horses we were used to riding.

Billy sat on her back for a little while, making sure she was broken to ride. He then gave her a little squeeze with his knees to get her going, and she did. She took off at full speed, leaving Billy sitting in the air before falling straight down.

I was the first to find out she could and would jump. There was a large ditch running through our pasture, and if the horse I was riding was trotting, it would always slow down and walk slowly across the ditch.

I got a real surprise when I approached the same ditch for the first time riding the mare. As soon as we reached the edge of the ditch, she didn't walk across, as a normal, sensible horse would - she jumped it.

Since we always rode bareback, it was not unusual for us to fall off if the horse did a quick and unexpected movement. Actually, quite often, we would fall off while the horse was standing perfectly still. I wasn't used to our horses jumping over a stick, much less a wide ditch.

I'm still not sure whether I fell directly into the ditch or if I rolled backwards into it from the other side. Either way, I must have hit the ground pretty hard because it took a while for me to figure out where I was and what exactly happened. When I finally was able to crawl out of the ditch, the mare had made it back to the barn and was looking in my direction, seemingly wondering why I wasn't still on her back.

We also found out the hard way that when she was running, she would occasionally slide to a stop. Her stops were similar to how rodeo horses would stop when a calf-roper lassoed a running calf.

She only skidded to a stop a couple of times while we were riding her, but each time, we went flying over her head. We never did figure out the code word or action that would cause her to throw on the brakes. But every time we rode her, we were concerned we might accidentally say or do something that would trigger her rapid braking.

Bow and Arrows

We would use flexible willow or other limber tree limbs to make bows for shooting arrows. A string was tied to one end of the limb, and then the limb was bent to form the bow. The other end of the string was then tied to the other end of the limb. Arrows were made from anything we could find that was fairly straight, such as large weeds or small tree limbs.

The finished bow and arrows were crudely made and obviously not very accurate, primarily because the arrows usually seemed to be bowed themselves.

We mostly shot our bows to see how high or far away the arrows would go. Either way, we did a lot of walking, retrieving our arrows, and lost most of them in the high weeds.

After a few minutes, we would tire of hunting arrows, or the string or bow would break, and we would move on to the next plaything.

Slingshots

Slingshots were made by cutting forks from tree branches, cutting up old inner tubes for the two stretch rubbers, and using the leather tongues out of old shoes for the pouch.

Many a time, we would not adequately secure the rubber to the fork, and when preparing to shoot, the rubber would come loose from the fork and fly backwards, hitting us in the face. That would really hurt, often bruising, or occasionally blackening an eye.

We mostly shot the slingshots at tin cans or fence posts, but now and then, we would shoot at each other. Every once in a while, we would aim at a bird, and it would have to move fast to avoid becoming a victim.

See-Saws

We usually used a large block of wood and a long board to make see-saws. After enjoying the peaceful ride for a while, we often began a competition by trying to throw the other off. We would either scoot to the very end of the board and then throw the other high in the air, or jerk the board sideways, trying to unbalance the other, causing them to fall off. Most of the time, the game ended with no one hurt, but occasionally, one of us would hit the ground hard enough to end up with bruises or aching elbows.

String Phones

We made play phones by using tin cans and a string. We first punched a small hole into the bottoms of two small cans. Then, each end of a long string, at least 50 feet long, was pushed through the hole of each can and knotted to keep it from pulling back out. We would then be able to talk to each other by talking and listening into the open ends of the cans.

The tighter we pulled the string, the louder the sound. We would sometimes further increase the sound level by coating the string with resin we could find on peach trees.

Of course, it didn't take long for us to tire of the talking game and move on to something different.

Wheelbarrows

Just about every time we found a small wheel with a hole suitable for an axle, we would make a wheelbarrow and take turns giving each other rides on it. The rides usually didn't last very long because either the wheelbarrow fell apart, or, for bonus fun, we would begin trying to dump the rider off. Either way, it was usually not long before someone was hurt or mad, or both.

Wheelbarrows were useful tools around the farm and we often used them to bring in wood for the night. We would stack the wood on the wheelbarrow and then push it to the back porch, where we would stack most of it, and then carry an armload or two inside and place it behind the stove.

Stilts

We made stilts, which we called "Walkers," by finding and cutting a small bush or tree branch with a relatively straight section about four feet long and having a limb branching out sideways to serve as a place for our feet. We left about a foot of the branch below the fork to create the desired height. The straight section above the fork served as the handle.

To make the stilts, we would first locate a saw and an axe and head to the woods. We would cut and try several variations before each of us found just the right size stilts to fit our feet.

Walking with the stilts was hard, especially in the hot sun of summer. It didn't take long for us to be covered with sweat and dirt from having fallen several times.

We didn't use straps to hold our feet on the stilts. We walked by lifting the handle and our foot at the same time and taking a step. That worked fairly well, unless we lifted our foot higher than we lifted the handle, or if the handle and the foot were not timed together.

Usually, after a few minutes, we had perfected walking with the stilts and kept at it until our bare feet were sore or blistered from the forks rubbing against our feet.

Popguns

Elderberry bushes were abundant in a field near our East View home. The branches and stems of Elderberry bushes are hollow and filled with a soft material called pith. That made them ideal for use in making popguns to shoot paper wads. Our paper wads were just pieces of paper we chewed until they were moist enough to be rolled into a tight ball.

We would push the pith out of a six or eight-inch straight section of an Elderberry branch to create the barrel. A push rod was made by trimming the bark off of a straight section of a hardwood tree limb and sizing it just slightly smaller in diameter and length than the Elderberry barrel.

To shoot the popgun, we squeezed a moistened paper wad into both ends of the barrel, inserted the pushrod behind the back wad of paper, and slammed the rod as fast as we could into the barrel. The wad of paper on the other end of the barrel would come out fast and make a loud popping sound. At close range, the paper wad would actually sting.

We sometimes found berries from trees, such as dogwood or sassafras, which were just the right size for use as ammunition instead of paper wads.

We often used the popguns as pistols and had gunfights. Since it took a little while to chew and moisten another paper wad and then reload, the person who shot first would often be in trouble. While the first shooter was still making a fresh paper wad, the other person would have time to dash forward and shoot the first shooter at point-blank range.

Elderberry bushes were prolific bearers of large berry pods. We erroneously believed that the elderberries contained poison and were not edible. That caused us to miss out on a lot of nutritious food.

Comic Books

When I was eight years old, I realized how much I enjoyed reading comic books. It didn't really matter what they were about, though Superman was probably my favorite. Sometimes, I would read the same one a dozen times. No matter how many times I read Superman, I would forget what I was supposed to be doing and enter his world of flying and fighting bad people.

Every time I got my hands on a comic I hadn't read before, I would plan to make it last a long time by reading just a few pages and then putting it down and doing something else. But I never could find a good place to stop. Instead, I would end up reading the whole thing almost as fast as I could flip the pages.

One of my aunts, living in Mt. Sterling, KY, had a son a few years older than me who also enjoyed comic books. He did odd jobs and actually spent most of his money buying new comics as soon as they became available. A couple of times a year, my aunt would come to visit, and when she did, she would bring a stack of his old comics and give them to us.

There was nothing like the excitement of getting not just one but a whole stack—maybe twenty comics - I hadn't read before. I would immediately head to the barn or another quiet place and start reading. If Mom hadn't called me to dinner or sent me to bed, I wouldn't have stopped until I had read them all.

After all of us had read those, we would trade them to our friends for others we hadn't read. A good comic book, such as Superman, could circulate for months and eventually pass through the hands of nearly every kid within the community.

Hunting

Beginning when I was around twelve years old, I enjoyed hunting rabbits and squirrels and would take home, or give to my grandparents, the few I was able to kill.

The only gun I ever used was a 22 single-shot rifle. Sometimes, I would see a squirrel run into a hole in a tree, and I would try to shoot it when it came back out. First, I had to find a good spot to sit down and then watch the hole, often for two to three hours, until the squirrel finally came out or I went nearly blind, whichever came first.

Nearly always, when the squirrel was ready to come out, he would first sit in the hole for ten or fifteen minutes with just his nose barely sticking out. Then, if everything seemed normal, he would venture the rest of the way out and sit on a limb near the hole for maybe three to five seconds before scurrying away. Those three to five seconds were what I had been waiting for, and they were my opportunity to take a shot at him.

Most of the time, I missed him because I could barely see after having stared at the hole for hours, or he saw my slight movements and darted back into his hole.

Mom would always try to buy a few apples and nuts for Christmas. However, I never ate all of my share of the apples, but always saved some for use as bait when setting rabbit snares. As far as I knew, apples were the only reasonable bait for rabbits.

I would set the snare by tying a string to a stout sapling and bending it over to form a noose at the other end. I would then cut and drive a small forked limb into the ground and use small sticks to make a trigger. A piece of apple would be attached to the trigger.

I would try to visit each trap at least once a day to see if I had caught a rabbit. It was always exciting to find a rabbit in one of my traps. I would take the rabbit home, and if Dad was too busy to prepare it for cooking, I would walk to my Granddad's house and give it to him. He never turned down a rabbit or squirrel and would immediately dress it and, in short order, would have it on the stove cooking.

Occasionally in late fall, Billy and I would go night hunting for opossums. We never ate them but intended to sell their hides. Ripe persimmons were a favorite food of opossums, so we would search every persimmon tree we knew of for miles around.

We were never all that excited about actually getting an opossum because they were difficult to skin, and the hides had to be stretched and dried for several weeks before they could be sold. They also had an offensive smell, making it hard to work with them. I believe the most we ever got for an opossum hide was 25 cents. The best thing about hunting opossums was the adventure of looking for them and helping ourselves to the ripe persimmons.

Sometimes, instead of selling the hide, we cut part of the hides into long shoe and boot strings. The strings were tough and would last a long time.

Every once in a while, I would hear someone talking of going snipe hunting. I had no idea what a snipe was, but catching them sounded like fun. A friend, a few years older than me, invited me to go snipe hunting one night with him and his older brother. They wanted me to bring a large sack and hold it open while they went off to find the snipe and drive them into the sack.

Luckily for me, Billy explained what they were planning. Instead of finding and driving Snipe into the bag, they would go home, leaving me waiting in the dark until I realized that I had been suckered. After Billy's insight, I thanked them, but said I had all the snipe I needed, and passed up the invite.

Snipe hunting was an old, handed-down trick or scam among rural residents, more fun to talk about than actually pull off. There were no such things as snipes in central Kentucky, but the success of the trick depended on the victim wanting to be included in an adventure, but unwilling to admit he didn't know what snipes were.

26

Sibling Disputes

Although my brothers and I generally got along, we still had our disputes — usually nothing more than shouting matches or grandiose threats. A few times, an argument escalated into a wrestling match, but those almost always ended before anyone landed a real blow.

I can't remember what most of those arguments were about; odds are they were over nothing, or something so trivial it would seem ridiculous today. More often, we relied on our well-worn verbal sparring to diffuse things. If Billy or Doug were annoying me, I might say, "Quit doing that," and they'd answer, "Make me." I'd come back, "If I'd made you, I'd have made you right." Or maybe I'd threaten, "Quit that or I'll kick you to Kingdom Come," and they'd snap, "Oh yeah — you and what army?" Those little exchanges usually did the trick and kept disagreements from turning into real fights.

The Short-Lived Cabin

One summer, Billy and I decided to build a small cabin in our woods and use sassafras trees about eight inches in diameter for the logs. Sassafras trees are tall with few limbs and are much less valuable than many other hardwoods. But most importantly, they were relatively easy to cut using a two-person cross-cut saw or even an axe. After felling and cutting them to the desired length, we began stacking them to form the cabin walls.

We made good progress by working on the cabin nearly all the time we weren't doing real work, such as taking care of the tobacco crop. Our walls had reached a height of about five feet when Billy suddenly got mad over something or other and tore the whole thing down.

That really upset me since we had put so much effort into building it. I went for him and tried to throw him to the ground. He fended me off two or three times, but I kept coming at him. He finally had to resort to pinning me to the ground until I decided to give up fighting him and get my revenge some other way.

As I was heading back to the house, I was still mad and decided a good way to get back at him was to use a stick of wood to bust the TV that we had bought with money earned by renting a tobacco patch.

But thankfully, by the time I got home, I realized that if I did that, it would hurt me and everyone else in the family just as much, or possibly even more, than Billy. I also began to realize I was tired of fooling with the cabin, and maybe tearing it down was not such a bad thing after all.

By the next day, the whole thing was forgotten, and we went on to some other project. Neither he nor I can remember what had upset him so much that day that he tore down what we had been working on for weeks. Maybe we had forgotten to include a door, or he had just gotten tired or bored of working on it, and decided to bring a swift end to the whole endeavor.

The Horse Bridle

Another time, when I was around 12 years old, Dad was getting ready to plow the tobacco and wanted to get it done before the rains came. He told Billy and me to get the horse, which happened to be on the other side of the field.

I happened to be standing closer to the horse's bridle, so I got it, and we headed to the back of the field to put the bridle on the horse and bring him back to the barn. But as soon as we got there, the horse decided he didn't want to plow that day and took off back towards the barn.

Since I had carried the bridle all the way to the back of the field to where the horse had been, I figured it was Billy's turn, and he should carry it back to the barn. He disagreed with my logic and said, "You brought it, you carry it back".

That didn't seem fair to me, so I threw it on the ground and headed back to the barn, thinking Billy would surely not let it just lie there without picking it up. But Billy, being a little stubborn, didn't pick it up, and we fussed and argued all the way back to the barn while leaving the bridle at the back of the field.

When we got back, Dad had the horse cornered in the barn and asked us to hand him the bridle. It really irritated him when we told him it was on the ground all the way at the back of the field.

My seemingly good explanation for leaving it there didn't seem to make as much sense to him. I believe he whacked me on the bottom and then went to do the same to Billy. But Billy didn't want any part of the punishment and took off running and completely disappeared.

He hadn't come home by dark, and both Mom and Dad began to worry about him. Early the next morning, Dad went to several houses, where he may have gone, asking if anyone had seen him. After a couple of nights, we received word that he was at our grandparents.

We went there, and sure enough, Billy was hiding in their barn. I think he had stayed a couple of nights at a friend's house, a mile or two from home, and then gone to our grandparents.

Dad was relieved that he was unhurt and promised him that if he came home, the whole incident would never be mentioned again. Billy decided that was the best deal he was likely to get and went home with us.

As far as I know, that was the end of it, as Dad kept his word and never mentioned the incident again.

Soon after Billy took off, I retrieved the bridle from the back of the field because I was now the only one who knew where it was.

I had mixed emotions about having to get it. I was mad at Billy for not carrying it back and at least a little regretful that my throwing it down had caused so much trouble.

Borrowing Doug's Bicycle

More than once, I had to hide from Doug until he cooled off. There was one time that I especially remember, and I probably deserved his anger. He had an old bicycle that he was especially proud of, and made sure I knew to leave it alone. If my bike was out of commission, I would sometimes borrow his - most of the time without his permission.

One time, while he was at the back of the house doing something or other, I decided to take it for a short ride down our driveway to check the mailbox. On the way back, I was really flying, trying to get there before he discovered I had taken his bike.

But he apparently saw me due to the dust cloud I was making on our gravel drive. Just before I reached the porch, I saw him coming around the house yelling at me, and about the same time, the bicycle chain came off, leaving me with no brakes. Before I could figure out what to do, I hit the porch at full speed and went flying over the handlebars onto the porch.

I landed hard, scattering mail, cats, buckets, and more than likely a few chickens all over the porch. The front wheel of his bike was knocked completely loose from the frame and went rolling around the house toward Doug.

While I was trying to decide how badly I was hurt, I looked up and saw Doug running toward me, carrying his front wheel over his head - ready to use it as a club. I immediately forgot about my pains from hitting the porch and got out of there in a hurry. Luckily, I could run faster than him, especially since he was carrying his heavy bicycle wheel.

After a few hours avoiding him, I figured I was safe and helped him put his bicycle back together. Thankfully, there was no real damage to the bike, me, or the chickens. I don't remember whether the mail eventually made it into the house.

After that little incident, I still occasionally "borrowed" his bike, but much less often than before the accident.

My Little Brother Evens the Score

Doug had a temper and an ability to carry a grudge that more than made up for his smaller size. Every once in a while, I would get into an argument or a push match with him. Most often, the argument was over Doug wanting to go with a friend and me when we would be going fishing or maybe swimming. The last thing we wanted was having to watch out for a smaller kid and possibly explain how he got lost, and we had left him in the woods.

It was hard to convince Doug to stay home and not follow us. I would try intimidating him by threatening to hit him with a stick or telling Mom about something he had done recently that would get him in trouble. It always took a while to discourage him, but eventually, he would give up and go back home.

If Mom felt I had been picking on Doug, she would tell me to be careful because someday, he might get bigger than me and get even. I tended to keep an eye on his growth rate, hoping that he wasn't catching up with me. He eventually did catch up, but by then, we both were essentially grown, and I guess he had decided to let me live.

But at least once, he did even the score a bit. When I was around ten or twelve years old, I came down with a severe kidney ailment called Bright's disease. Treatment was complete bed rest for at least six weeks in a darkened room with no excitement and a complete lack of salt in my food. The objective was to keep my blood pressure as low as possible. I was not allowed out of bed except to use a pot beside the bed.

All my chores, while I was sick, fell onto my brothers' shoulders, which, after a few weeks, started getting on their nerves. They were further aggravated when, during severe thunderstorms, Mom would have Dad carry me into the living room so I could lie on the couch for a while. This obvious special treatment added to Doug's frustration with me.

I admit I also may have sometimes overplayed my hand by asking Mom for special treats. She would explain to the others that I was really sick, and this would help me get better. When Mom wasn't looking, and to reduce my boredom, I would wave the treat at Doug. After about four or five weeks of this, Doug blew a gasket and decided something had to be done.

While everyone else, except my four-year-old sister, Juanita, was working in the garden, he seized the opportunity and began beating me with a broom, starting while I was sound asleep. It didn't take long for me to wake up and realize I was in trouble. I was cornered, and about all I could do was curl up, dive beneath the bed covers, and try to fend off the broom strikes.

Luckily, Juanita was old enough to know this was probably not a good thing and probably should be stopped. She went for help, but by the time Mom understood what she was trying to say, got there, and stopped him, he was getting pretty tired of whacking me with the broom.

I wasn't really hurt because the heavy quilts on the bed protected me, but it did create more excitement than I had for weeks.

He probably got into more trouble over that than I ever knew, but the beating did work, and I was ready to sign a peace treaty. After that, I was more careful in asking for special treatment, or at least, made sure he wasn't around when I did.

A positive side effect of being in bed so long was that I learned some books were actually interesting to read. I had never voluntarily read a book all the way through. Mom gave me a book called "Huckleberry Finn", probably trying to keep me quiet for a while. After finishing it, I actually asked for more books. However, if someone stopped in to see if I was still alive, I would hide them under the bedcovers. I didn't want word to get out to my friends that I read books without even having to.

The six weeks of bed confinement finally ended, and I was allowed to slowly begin getting out of bed and back to being more or less normal again. But the memory of that beating with a broom stayed with me for months, causing me to stop and think before mistreating Doug.

27

Mom's Spin the Chicken Trick

One summer, we left our young son and daughter with my parents for about a week while my wife and I were traveling. During their stay, Mom decided to fix a chicken for lunch and, with my kids' help, had somehow managed to catch one. That was no small feat, as the chickens were allowed to roam free, and getting one cornered to catch it was almost impossible.

After the chase, the kids sat down on a nearby bench watching her hold the chicken and being obviously proud that they caught it. They were wondering what would happen next now that the chicken had been caught.

Without thinking to warn the kids to close their eyes or look away, Mom did her famous "spin the chicken by the head" trick – something between a magic trick and a scene from a Hitchcock movie.

Before my kids could even blink, Mom was standing there holding the chicken's head in her hand while the chicken was running a short distance across the yard before falling over. My kids' eyes and mouths were wide open as they tried to figure out what happened.

Although Mom performed that little circus trick at least 50 years ago, my kids still talk and laugh about sitting there waiting to see what Mom was going to do with the chicken they had helped catch. They got an answer they were not expecting.

As I was growing up, Mom occasionally shared memories of having to work long hours in the tobacco and corn fields as a child and teenager. When talking of those times, she seemed to hold a slight grudge against her father for making her work so hard in the fields, feeling as though he treated her more like a son than his daughter.

I suspect he had no choice, because he was trying to feed nine kids on a small hillside farm in the Appalachian Mountains of Eastern Kentucky, which would have been especially hard or nearly impossible during the great depression.

My grandfather told of using his own mules during the great depression and working long days pulling logs out of the steep hillsides for 50 cents a day.

As in most households, Mom held our family together. It was she who sat up with us when we were sick and made sure we had clothes to wear, were clean when we went to school, and had food on the table when we were hungry.

She not only cooked and kept house, but heated water in a large tub over a wood fire in the backyard and hand scrubbed our dirty clothes on a washboard.

She would then rinse the clothes in a separate tub and tightly twist the wet clothes to get as much water out as possible. We later obtained a hand-cranked clothes wringer that made getting most of the water out of the clothes much easier.

She would then hang all the clothes on a clothesline to dry. After they had dried, she would bring them in and iron the shirts using heavy, solid metal irons heated by sitting them on top of our hot wood stove.

One of Mom's Old Irons

She usually had two or three irons heating at the same time, so she wouldn't have to stop ironing to reheat the iron. Since we didn't have electricity for steam irons, she would sprinkle the clothes using her fingers to dip water from a jar. That way the hot iron made its own steam as she moved it back and forth across the shirt.

Around 1950, my grandparents purchased a gas engine-powered washing machine. It did a reasonably good job of washing the clothes, but the motor smoked badly, and keeping it running, fixing water leaks, and refilling the gas tank turned out to be harder than expected. After using it for a few weeks, they abandoned it and went back to washing clothes by hand.

During the heat of summer and without air conditioning, Mom picked vegetables from the garden and canned them over a hot wood fire in the kitchen. She also picked blackberries, apples, and peaches, and canned those as well. The list of work items just keeps going, including churning milk to make butter, keeping house, and washing dishes. All of this work was accomplished while serving as cook and nurse, preparing school lunches, and working outside in the garden and yard. She also helped strip the tobacco and occasionally milked two or three cows when we were sick.

To get a little extra cash, Mom would sell the cream she had separated from our milk. I don't remember all the ways she separated it, but early on, I believe she simply let the whole milk sit overnight, and then carefully dipped off the cream. Later, we had a cream separator that made the separation task much easier. The milk was poured into the separator, which was really a small tank with a sight gauge on the side and a valve at the bottom. After the cream had separated and floated to the top of the milk, the milk was first removed by opening the valve and letting the milk drain into a container, leaving the cream in the separator. The cream was then drained into a separate container.

After a few days, Mom would have a couple of gallons of cream that she kept from spoiling by lowering it into the well. When ready, she would tell Billy and me to take it to a local grocery store and sell it. We would put a long tobacco stick under the handle of the container to share the weight and carry it about two miles to the store.

The butterfat content was measured by the owner of the store, who would then pay us about $1.50 for the two gallons of cream. We would then use the money from the cream to buy an item or two Mom needed, such as sugar or coffee.

Although I don't remember having any major incidents with the cream on the long walks to the store, there must have been several minor ones. There is no way Billy and I could have carried the cream that far without, at least once, one of us dropping one end of the stick. I am sure Mom knew to tighten the lid tightly, or she might not have had much cream left by the time we arrived at the store.

Mom's Parents and Siblings – First Row Left: Buel, Pa, Ma, Zelda - Standing Left: Ed, Lee, Cora (Mom), Marie, Paul, Earl – Not shown: Ervin

We didn't mind carrying the cream to the store, as it got us out of the tobacco patch for a while, plus there was always something interesting going on around the stores.

Mom always kept a few hens for laying eggs and to provide an occasional chicken dinner. We usually used all the eggs, but sometimes, we had a few extra, and we would sell them along with the cream.

A chicken became a prime candidate for the dinner table if Mom determined one of her hens was not laying regularly or nesting somewhere other than in the chicken house.

When ready to cook the chicken for lunch or supper, Mom would have us corner and catch it for her. She would then wring its neck and begin the long process of preparing it for our meal.

Mom's primary plant decoration in the kitchen was usually a sweet potato vine growing in the window. She would put a sweet potato in a partially filled glass of water and set it on the windowsill to get some sunlight. After a week or two, the sweet potato would sprout and begin growing a long, bushy vine. She would watch over it all summer, making sure the glass always had at least some water, and trimming the vines to prevent them from taking over the whole wall. During winter, the kitchen was too cold at night for the vine, so Mom would toss it out and start over in the spring.

Mom was deathly afraid of storms, especially when there was lightning. She had known someone in the community who had been killed by lightning, and to make matters worse, Mom had been in our yard near a tree when lightning struck the tree. She was knocked down and briefly blinded by the strike. After that, if Dad was not home and a dark cloud came up, she would start worrying that we were going to get blown away.

Many a time, she rounded us up and headed across the field to my uncle's house. They had a below-ground cellar, and if the storm appeared bad enough, all of us would get in it. Just being with another adult during the storm made Mom feel safer.

Since it usually took five minutes or more to rush across the open field, we were in far greater danger by being out in the open during an approaching storm than if we had just stayed home. But our arguments that we should just stay inside and not head across the field seemed to fall on deaf ears.

Mom usually wanted us kids to attend church and bible school, but the nearest church was about five miles away, over on Highway 84. Actually, there were two churches of different denominations – Presbyterian and Methodist, located right across the street from each other. Neither church had enough members to make it totally viable on its own, so all attendees agreed to take turns alternating attendance at both churches. One Sunday, everyone attended the Presbyterian Church and then the next week, everyone attended the Methodist Church. The Ministers of both churches served on a part-time basis.

She wanted Dad to drive us to church, but he usually refused except for a few times on special occasions and at night during revivals. Dad would attend the revivals, but never went to the front of the church when the minister made the invitation. Many of the kids remained outside playing and generally making a nuisance of themselves by playing a noisy game of tag, in the dark, while the revivals were going on.

Mom could drive, but seldom did, as it made her nervous. But she decided church was too important to pass up, so she decided to drive us herself and did for quite a while.

However, one Sunday, we were leaving church, and Mom accidentally pulled in front of a car while entering the highway. Thankfully, no one was seriously injured, although our car was not drivable. We waited in our car while someone went by our home and let Dad know about the wreck.

Dad had my uncle Ervin drive him to where we were waiting, and then to tow our car home. The other person's car was only slightly damaged and still drivable. Dad paid to have the other person's car repaired, and used hammers and pullers to fix our car the best he could.

For a long time afterwards, Mom was even more nervous about driving and kept wondering why someone who had just been attending church could have such a bad thing happen to them.

It seemed Mom always had a broom within her reach. In addition to using it as a cleaning tool, she used it as a weapon against chickens on the porch and sometimes as a threat against misbehaving or rowdy kids. All of us, except maybe Juanita, had at one time or another felt the broom against our back-sides. Due to so much use, they didn't last long, and she was always needing another one.

One year, she somehow got the idea of making her own brooms to both save money and make sure she had plenty of backups. She had Dad plant several rows of broom corn near our tobacco patch. The broom corn grew well, giving Mom plenty of raw material for her brooms.

However, she never mastered the technique of properly tying the broom corn into recognizable and functional brooms. Every time she used one of her brooms, she would leave a trail of stems that had to also be swept up. After a few more tries at putting together a better broom, she gave up, and Dad plowed under the remaining broom corn stalks.

The government used to give away certain food commodities to needy families as a way of increasing demand and prices that farmers received for their farm products. A government office in E-town began a monthly giveaway of cheese, peanut butter, and a couple of other products, depending on availability and need for price support. All you had to do was provide some proof of need, such as an income tax return, sign up, and then each month go and pick up the items.

Dad was reluctant to go get the free items because it seemed like a welfare program to him. He was probably a little embarrassed, plus it hurt his pride to have someone hand him the food. However, he did agree to drive Mom if she would actually go in to get the food. Mom knew we kids could use it, and lost no time in signing up for the giveaway program.

The food also gave Mom some well-deserved relief from worrying about us possibly running out of food and not having enough to eat. The cheese came in five-pound boxes and usually lasted us the full month between government giveaways. We participated in the food program for approximately two years. I don't know whether the program ended or we simply grew tired of making the monthly trips to E-town.

Mom was subject to what now seems to have been panic attacks, possibly brought on by stress. She would occasionally find it almost impossible to breathe. That would obviously scare her and increase her overall stress level. A few times, she actually turned a noticeably darker color, apparently due to the lack of oxygen.

One summer, she was especially vulnerable to the attacks and most of the time, unable to cook and clean the house. Although I was only around twelve years old at the time, Dad said if I stayed near the house and helped Mom, he and my brothers would take care of everything else. I agreed as it would get me out of having to milk each morning and night - a job I hated.

Although I only learned how to cook green beans and corn bread, and maybe one or two other items, no one ever complained. They were likely afraid I would quit, leaving everyone on their own. With plenty of milk and garden stuff, we really didn't need much cooked food. We made it through the summer, and the much-needed rest helped Mom reduce the number and severity of the attacks.

Mom often had a quilting frame hanging from the living room ceiling near the center of the room so she could easily reach all four edges of the quilt. Although we needed the quilts, I believe she enjoyed quilting them as it would get her mind temporarily off her many worries. Sometimes my grandmother or other women would help with one of the quilts.

She was especially passionate about dolls and had a huge collection. After we grew up and had left home, all of us would buy dolls for her birthday and for Christmas. It didn't matter whether we got her an expensive one from Macy's or for fifty cents from a Goodwill store - she liked them all. One bedroom where I slept when visiting was crammed full of dolls of all sizes. It felt a little strange to wake up in the middle of the night and see the many dolls (some at least three feet tall) lined up around the walls staring at me.

Sometime after Dad died, Mom moved to Benton, KY, to be near my sister Juanita. Her new home had a large backyard with a small pear tree. Each year, when the pears ripened, the squirrels would start harvesting them and kept at it until none were left.

Mom found a cap pistol someone had left at her house. She would watch, and when she saw the squirrels begin to steal the pears, she would get the cap pistol and fire at them from her back porch. I am not sure what the neighbors thought since the cap pistol looked and sounded a little like a real gun - very loud.

I know I would have been a little concerned if I were the neighbor who lived just behind her backyard and in the direct line of fire. I tried to get her to stop doing that, but she was too annoyed at the squirrels to give it up. I finally confiscated the cap pistol without telling her - putting an end to the squirrel war. She probably guessed where it went.

After she died, as I did with Dad, I created a small collage of several of Mom's treasures and personal items. These included a small doll, sewing tools, pencils, and eyeglasses. I also included the cap pistol and a box of caps for the cap pistol she used to shoot at the squirrels. Future generations will probably wonder why the cap pistol and caps were included. Maybe they will read this book and then understand.

28

The Rock House

A long, steep land drop-off with a creek at the bottom was located about a mile from our house and was part of our Big Clifty property. There is a natural, large cave-like opening

View from Outside the Rock House

eight to ten feet above the creek, and into the solid rock cliff known as "The Rock House". The floor and ceiling are both flat, solid rock, probably having been carved out by water over millions of years. A small waterfall plunges over the cliff and onto the floor of the Rock House before draining down into the creek. You have to walk behind or through the waterfall when going into the Rock House.

Apparently, American Indians used the Rock House extensively as a permanent home – it is big enough for several families or even an entire small community. A round hole, twelve inches deep and six inches wide, has been carved into the solid rock floor for use in pounding and grinding corn.

A level area of several acres with rich topsoil, immediately across the creek and directly in front of the Rock House,

View from Inside the Rock House

would have been ideal for growing corn. One could fish while sitting on the floor of the Rock House by dangling the feet over the edge, and dropping a fishing line straight down into the creek.

Countless numbers of people have enjoyed camping and fishing there, including us boys. We spent a lot of time there exploring and just hanging out. We would build a fire, set out fishing poles, and search the area for arrowheads which used to be plentiful in and near the Rock House.

We didn't have to worry about rain or storms, so we would just throw an old quilt directly onto the level rock surface, roll up in it, and sleep soundly.

I remember one night, we didn't get to go to sleep right away. We had picked a different section of the Rock House to build our fire, and after rolling up in our quilts, wasps began falling on us. They had built their nests in small cracks in the ceiling directly above us, and smoke from the fire had driven them out, causing them to fall on us.

We found several tomahawks, axes, spearheads, and arrowheads at the Rock House and picked up many more from nearby plowed fields. I have no idea what happened to them. Likely, many of them are still in the woods somewhere near the Rock House, lying where we laid them down to swing on a grape vine or climb a tree to pick wild grapes.

While camping in the Rock House, I often thought about how much fun it would be to use a small boat and see how far I could go by just floating down the creek, starting at the Rock House. I often wondered whether I could make it all the way to the Mississippi River or if waterfalls and rapids would block my route. I guess I had read that Huckleberry Finn book at least once too many times.

29

Close Encounters

We had lots of opportunities to get hurt on the farm, especially since we were so often working with and around horses and heavy equipment. But most of the time when we got hurt really bad or had a close call, it was when we were simply doing everyday routine things or doing something we shouldn't have been doing in the first place. We knew how dangerous the horses were and kept our guard up, helping to prevent major accidents.

Billy's School Bus Accident

While I was in the first grade at Lynnvale School, the school bus would occasionally be late in arriving back at school to pick us up. Since classes were already over, students would be waiting outside near where the bus usually stopped. As it pulled up near the boarding point, a lot of pushing and shoving went on, trying to be first onto the bus. I have no idea why that mattered, as there were plenty of seats for everyone and usually the same people sat together anyway. But there was something about being first onto an empty bus and having first choice of seats.

One afternoon, Billy, who was around eight at the time, was either at or near the front of the line and was somehow pushed down and fell under the bus while it was still slowly rolling towards the usual boarding area. Before he could scramble out from under the bus, the dual back wheels ran over his legs just above the knees.

As he was yelling and screaming, the school principal grabbed him up and immediately took him to a doctor in Elizabethtown, about ten to fifteen miles away. At that time, the nearest hospital was in Louisville, nearly 40 miles away. After they had left and the excitement died down, everyone else, including me, got on the bus and went home.

By the time I had gotten off the bus and completed the long walk to our house, it was much later than when Billy and I usually got home. Mom was waiting for us and saw that Billy was not with me. Naturally, she asked, "Where's Billy"? I told her, "He got run over by the bus". Needless to say, my simplistic but straightforward answer created considerable excitement. After some frantic questioning, all I could tell her was that I didn't know how badly hurt he was, but he was screaming a lot. We didn't have a phone, so Mom had no way of finding out his condition.

She and Dad rushed to the school. They then took off for Elizabethtown, and all the way there, they still had no idea how badly he was hurt or if he was even still alive.

Billy was not critically injured and somehow didn't even have broken bones. Apparently, the flat surface of the school driveway prevented greater damage to his legs.

All the doctor could do was treat the bruises and cuts and tell him to stay off his feet for a couple of weeks. After a few days, he was up and moving around pretty much as usual, but he has some lingering issues with his legs and knees even to this day.

Mom and Dad were really upset with the school and let them know it.

After the incident, the school policy was changed, requiring all kids to remain in the classrooms until all buses were completely stopped and ready for boarding.

Looking back, it was an accident just waiting to happen and could have easily been fatal.

I am not sure just how safety-conscious the school was, even after Billy's accident. My uncle, who was only a few years older than me, lived at the end of a long school bus route - approximately 12 miles from the school. While still in high school and at the age of 17, he was allowed to drive the school bus that served that long, winding route from his home to school. He was mature for his age and was able to maintain order on the bus. Also, he never had an incident or accident with the bus, even when driving in wintry conditions.

As far as I know, none of the parents complained about a high school student driving the bus. More than likely, most didn't even know it.

I doubt a high school student would be allowed to drive a school bus today.

Billy seems to have more lives than a cat. In addition to having a school bus run over him, he had several other serious accidents while growing up, including breaking his arms, falling out of the back of trucks, and the like. His accidents and narrow escapes have continued into his adult life and include being run over with a bulldozer, falling out of a tractor bucket onto his head, having a tornado destroy his home, having his pants catch on fire while operating a tractor, accidentally shooting himself in the foot, and burning his house to the ground while trying to clean a pot of grease.

The Unlucky Chicken

One day, when I was about 12 years old, I was on our front porch playing with the slingshot I had just made, and decided to see how far I could shoot it. I shot a couple of times at a fence post, then spotted some chickens down at the barn about 200 feet away.

The chickens were just walking around and scratching at the ground in front of the barn, looking for kernels of corn and other things spilled or left over from feeding the livestock. I began to wonder if the slingshot would reach close enough to the chickens to scare them.

I found a fairly round rock about half an inch in diameter and selected one of the chickens to serve as my target. Since the chicken was so far away, I pulled as hard as I could on the slingshot and shot at about a 45-degree angle and generally in the direction of the chicken.

I was expecting to get no closer to it than about 50 feet, but was hoping that after the rock hit the ground, it would continue rolling toward the chicken and cause it to jump or run away. I watched the rock sail upwards and start its descent while the chicken kept moving and pecking at the ground, completely oblivious to the oncoming rock.

Then, as the rock kept getting closer to the chickens, I began to worry just a little. Suddenly, the target chicken stopped and looked up, and then fell over and was completely still - no flopping or flapping of wings. It just lay there as still as the rock that had hit it. Apparently, the rock had hit the chicken dead center on the top of her head.

I looked around to make sure no one saw what I did, and then headed for the barn, wondering how I would explain this without getting in big trouble. I finally decided that, apparently, no one else saw it happen, so why should I bother them with the story? The chicken was only 1 out of about 20 we had, and surely wouldn't be missed. Telling about it would likely get me in trouble, and the chicken would still be dead.

But by the time I reached the barn, the chicken had almost come to its senses and was struggling to get up. I set it on its feet, and shortly, it wobbled away. I kept an eye on it for the next day or two just to be sure it was ok and hadn't died.

Later on, the chicken seemed to be in perfectly good shape, and as far as I know, continued to lay eggs as usual. As with most things like that, I decided I probably shouldn't try that again.

Close Call with the Buzz Saw

It was a hot day in September, and Billy and I had just gotten home from school. We changed out of our school clothes and were now getting ready to cut wood. Neither of us had on a shirt or shoes, which is the way we usually worked during the summer.

Dad was working in Louisville, but the night before had told us that after school, use the buzz saw and cut up the pile of poles that had been dragged up earlier.

Our buzz saw was a large, circular saw blade, close to three feet in diameter, mounted on a frame and driven by a flat belt connected to a tractor. Dad had obtained the saw shortly after buying a used John Deere tractor that had a drive pulley mounted on the side of the tractor.

It was called a buzz saw because the cutting edges were moving so fast that they made a buzzing sound as they rotated.

Since we didn't have a chainsaw, the buzz saw was the next best thing to make quick work of cutting long wooden poles into firewood length blocks of wood. The blade spun at high speed in the open air, usually with no guard, making it an impressive but extremely dangerous piece of equipment.

Buzz saws were notoriously dangerous, and accidents frequently occurred. They were likely the most dangerous piece of equipment on any farm or industrial site of that time period. Just about anything, such as a temporary loss of balance, slipping on ice or mud, or even tripping over a piece of the sawn wood, could cause someone to fall into the blade. There were no safety shields, emergency shut-offs, or protective clothing in those days—only the operator's caution stood between safety and disaster.

Many rural communities could tell stories of people—sometimes children—losing fingers, hands, or worse to the buzz saw. We didn't know it at the time, but the saw was the same type that Johnny Cash's brother fell into as a child and was killed.

Although dangerous, it really sped up the cutting of wood. While we were still in the woods, we would cut limbs and small trees into long poles. We then dragged the poles near the barn where the saw was located and used the saw to cut the limbs into firewood lengths. Just thinking about that saw, being so big, rotating so fast, and without any protection, gives me goosebumps. We had to stand about a foot from the rotating saw while lifting long, heavy poles onto the saw carriage. We then used the carriage to push the wood into the saw. The saw would eat through the wood faster than we could feed it. Our hands would be only inches from the blade when holding the wood.

Although we both were experienced with dangerous equipment, we had to be extremely careful to avoid an accident. It would have been so easy to get a hand cut off or possibly trip over all the wood lying around and fall into the saw. Luckily, Billy and I were never hurt while using the saw, but we did have a few close calls – most involving tripping as we struggled lifting the heavy poles onto the carriage.

The drive belt was also dangerous as it was stretched at least ten feet between the saw and the tractor with no guards or other protection. It could easily catch a piece of someone's clothing and jerk them into the saw or sever a hand or finger if accidentally caught under the belt.

When operating the saw, we were usually careful, but one day, after an hour or so of cutting wood, I began to get tired and wasn't nearly as watchful as I should have been. I reached around the saw to hold a piece of wood that hadn't been cut completely through. Just as my hand closed around it, the saw grabbed the wood. I was probably pulling on the stick of wood and may have caused it to bind against the high-speed blade.

Old "Buzz Saw" Just Like the One Billy and I Used as Young-sters (Photo Courtesy of Purple Wave Auction)

The next thing I knew, the stick of wood had been thrown outward by the saw and hit me full force on my shoulder and then the side of my head. I stumbled and could have fallen toward the saw, but luckily, I fell in the opposite direction.

Other than a knot on my head, I was fine. It was probably fortunate that the saw threw the stick of wood rather than pulling it into the saw. It might have pulled me or my arm along with the piece of wood.

We decided not to tell anyone how close I came to getting hurt because if Mom knew, she would insist we immediately stop using the saw and would never let us use it again. More than likely, she had no idea just how dangerous the saw really was, and Billy and I were not going to tell her, because it made cutting firewood so much easier than using a crosscut saw and axe.

Horses Don't Like Teasing

One day, I was apparently bored and began aggravating one of our horses as he was trying to eat just outside the barn. I was using a stick and kept pushing his ears of corn away, making him walk around after the corn. After a few minutes of this, I could tell he was getting disturbed, but I kept at it. Suddenly, he got tired of my little game, laid his ears back on his head, and came for me. I was only a few feet from him, so I knew it was time to get out of there and fast.

Luckily, I was standing in front of the hallway of the barn and dashed inside. I don't know how I did it, but I climbed the vertical wooden wall of the hallway and was eight or ten feet high in less than a second. A squirrel couldn't have gone up it faster than I did. I knew I had pushed him too far, and unless I got out of reach fast, I was done for.

He actually tried to reach me but couldn't, so he soon gave up and went back to eating. Needless to say, I was cautious around him for a long time and never teased him again.

I have no idea how I got up that wall so quickly. The horse, being right behind me and mad as a hornet, seems to have provided sufficient motivation. I have no doubt that if he could have reached me, he would have pulled me down or at least taken a large bite out of me.

30

Honing My Trading Skills

I used to really like trading things with other kids. The purpose of the trade wasn't to get something better but just different. I would keep whatever I had gotten for a little while, then tire of it and trade it for something else at the first opportunity.

I believe the first trade I ever made was when I was in second grade and attending the one-room school. I had found a mouse nest in the barn that had three or four very small newborn mice in it. The mice were pink and only about a half inch long, with their eyes still closed. I took them to school to show them around to the other kids.

For some reason, the other kids thought they were baby squirrels, and I didn't bother to correct them - that sounded better than mice. I guess I figured that would make my find even more interesting to everyone else. I do admit I was a little vague about where I found them.

I wasn't even thinking about a trade, but this one kid had a small pocketknife and offered it to me in trade for the "squirrels". At that point, I didn't want to admit they were mice and agreed to the trade. I figured they would die before he found out what they really were anyway.

It didn't take long after he got home for his parents to recognize what they really were and kill them. The next day, they sent a note to the teacher telling her what I had done and to make me return the knife. By then, I was sort of expecting that to happen, and so I handed over the knife while pleading innocence in knowing what they really were.

During another trade, I had received a multi-shot 22 rifle and a nice guitar, and really didn't intend to trade them away. Everyone who saw them, including my grandparents, bragged on me for having made such a good trade.

The guitar had a great sound and was occasionally borrowed for use during a local radio musical hour. But, as usual, after I had owned them for a while, I grew anxious for my next trade. I got caught up in the moment and probably made the worst trade anyone ever made.

For both the rifle and the guitar, I received several parts from an old broken lawn mower engine, a goat that had disappeared but with the promise it would return home in a couple of days, and a pet raccoon.

I believe the old lawn mower engine parts were what I really wanted, as I hadn't messed with small engines before. I could just imagine the possibilities of having a cylinder block and a piston. I was pretty sure I would, in no time at all, be able to put a complete engine together and use it to drive washing machines, clothes wringers, a go-cart, and just about anything else. Anyone who saw it in operation would surely brag about my excellent trade.

I wasn't able to do anything with the few parts of the engine I had. Instead, the parts lay around under a large tree in the front yard with grass growing up around them.

Mostly they were just lying around in Dad's way, so he eventually threw them in a junk pile. The goat never came back home, so I didn't even get to see it or even know for sure that it ever existed, and there were several times that I thought Mom was going to kill me over the damage caused by the raccoon.

The people who had bragged on my earlier trades now wondered if I had lost my mind. I began thinking the same thing.

The raccoon liked shiny things and would sneak into the house to steal forks, spoons, and even pocket watches, and then hide them in the barn or somewhere never to be seen again. If you were sitting down and not paying attention, it would even search your pockets and grab anything that it found, such as a knife or coins, and take off with them. It also seemed to really enjoy climbing curtains and tearing them down. It must have liked the fuss Mom made about the curtains being damaged.

Mom finally got fed up with the raccoon and gave me a very clear ultimatum - either the raccoon or I had to go, and she would let me choose.

I sold the raccoon to a man working on the road for eight dollars. I don't remember what I did with the eight dollars, but after spending it, there was nothing left of my trade – no engine, no goat, and no raccoon. Also, I now had no multi-shot rifle or fine guitar.

I still have an antique wind-up Victrola, with lots of old records, that I obtained in another trade with a neighbor boy.

My Raccoon Eating an Ear of Corn on Our porch

I am not sure what I traded for it, but it could have been an old bicycle I half-way fixed up, or maybe even a real pet squirrel I had raised after finding it in a tree nest. I had traded for the Victrola with the intent of taking it apart and using some of the parts, such as the springs and wind-up motor, to build something else. I had no use for a working Victrola but was fascinated by the workings of the springs and rotating mechanisms. But Mom protected it and wouldn't let me take it apart. She must have realized the Victrola's value and kept it away from me until I eventually gave up the idea of destroying it.

Vintage Victrola I Traded for as a Youngster

Thanks to her, I still have it and have collected many additional old records over the years

31

Making Bad Decisions

I was certainly no stranger to having made bad decisions when young. A lot of things sounded like good ideas at the time, but didn't turn out exactly as I planned.

My Short Boxing Career

While I was a sophomore in high school, the school decided to hold a fundraiser with multiple events, including student boxing matches. My friend Edward and I volunteered to be contestants and box each other. Actually, he volunteered for both of us and didn't mention it to me until word was out that we had signed up.

As the event approached, I began to worry a little about the match-up with Edward, because he was a little larger and more athletic. He also appeared even bigger and stronger as the event got closer.

I thought about just cancelling out, but didn't want to appear afraid. Besides, the brochure advertising the events had already been printed.

I also considered talking to Edward to see if we could come to an understanding about taking it easy on each other during the bout. After all, the bouts were for raising school funds, and we didn't get anything for all our efforts except possibly humiliation.

I gave up that idea as too risky, because, even though he was a friend, I didn't trust him to honor the agreement once in the ring. He might want to show some girl how good a boxer he was and really beat me. The only other option I could think of, which seemed to make sense at the time, was that I had to get in better shape before the event.

It was fall, and soon we would need firewood, so I decided to kill two birds with one stone. I planned to build up my stamina and muscle strength by cutting firewood over the weekend and each afternoon after school. I figured I would get the most benefit by using only an axe – no saws.

By the time I developed my plan and actually started cutting the wood, it was the last weekend before the boxing match on the following Friday night. I only had a few days to get in shape, but if I stuck with my plan, then that should be enough. Anyway, that was all the time left before the match, and I had to make the best of it.

All Saturday and Sunday, I used the ax and chopped down small trees and cut them into long poles that we could later cut to firewood length using our large tractor-driven saw. I worked until dark each day, then would do my share of the milking in the dark. Mom and the others were wondering what I was doing and asking, "Why are you working so hard cutting wood?" I would answer, "I want to get a head start on cutting firewood, and now seems a good time to start."

The following week, immediately after school, I would change clothes, grab the axe, and head for the woods. I started getting tired and really sore all over early in the week, but kept after it. I knew I had to get in shape or I was likely going to suffer the consequences in the boxing ring.

My last day of cutting wood was Thursday, and by that time, I had almost enough poles that, once sawn up, would probably last us the entire winter. But also by then, I was so worn out, I could barely swing the axe.

I was glad my stamina-building effort was finally complete. Friday, the day of the event, I had a hard time staying awake in class and just wanted to go somewhere and lie down.

When it was time for our boxing match, I put on the gloves but could hardly raise my arms, much less keep them up. I was sore all over and probably barely able to stand up.

We went through the motions with the match, but Edward must have sensed that something was wrong and asked, "Are you sick?" I faked a light cough and said, "I'm ok."

I was surprised, but he actually did take it easy on me during all three rounds, and the only damage to me was a bloody lip. The match was scored a draw, and I felt pretty good about that until I noticed all the matches were being scored a draw.

After a few days, the blisters on my hands had healed, and I was pretty much back to normal. However, I was sure my boxing career was over.

I learned the hard lesson that building stamina and muscle strength probably takes a little longer than a week. A positive outcome was that it gave us a good start on the winter's firewood.

Surviving Milking Time

I have never understood how a cow can kick you while milking her if you are standing or squatting in front of and out to the side of her kicking leg. It seems to me a cow should only be able to kick backwards – not forwards or sideways.

A few times, I thought we must have a target pinned on us to make it easier for them to score a direct hit.

Unlike the Walton's on TV, we didn't sit on little stools or chairs while milking. We just leaned over or squatted down. We mostly did that so we could beat a hasty retreat if one of the cows decided to try to kick us to kingdom come while we were milking her. Usually, if she kicked, she would either get us or the milk bucket, or both, because they could kick lightning fast. A cow's kick is so fast, I believe it would put a rattlesnake's strike to shame. I have been kicked in the leg, the chest, and even my arm. Neither Billy nor I was ever kicked in the head – or if we were, we don't remember it. We just tried making sure our heads were not within range of her foot.

We were taught responsibility and teamwork without even knowing it. For instance, we always had two or three cows that needed milking in the morning and late afternoon. The milk was an essential part of each meal as it was used not only for drinking, but for making butter and bread, and part of the cream was sold to provide a little extra cash.

Dad gave Billy and me the responsibility for milking, and as far as I know, he never had to remind us of when it was time to milk. We knew it was our decision - we could finish the milking before dark, or we could keep putting it off and have to find the cows and milk them in the dark. We always got it done, seldom having to milk in the dark.

When we occasionally milked after dark, and there was a bright moon, we would take the milk buckets with us to find the cows. We would then attempt to milk them there in the field instead of taking the time to drive them back to the darker barn. Most of the time, though, it would have been much quicker and easier to drive them to the barn because at least one or two of them would keep moving around trying to graze while we milked. We had to keep following them all over the field to finish milking, and usually ended up spilling most of it.

We would swear we would never do that again, but soon forgot how much trouble that had been and tried it again later with the same results.

The worst part of milking was that it had to be done twice a day - morning and night. But it wasn't too bad in the summer except for flies. Flies were all over the cows, and they were frequently switching their tails and slinging their heads, trying to scare them off. We had to be careful when milking to avoid being hit in the face with the end of her tail. That was very annoying and could actually hurt, especially if the tail was wet or partially frozen.

We always had one cow that was much more difficult to milk than the others. She wouldn't stand still or was more likely to kick the milk bucket or whoever was milking her. Once, when Billy was milking her outside the barn and on a little bank near the pond, she kicked him, and both Billy and the bucket just barely missed rolling into the pond. On another occasion, she kicked at me, and her foot went into the bucket of milk, splashing warm milk all over me and ruining the morning's milk. The cats had a feast of milk that morning.

Billy and I decided who milked that cow through threats or by making a trade. It was up to us to make the decision and get it done. I always milked her first when it was my turn. I just wanted to get it over as soon as possible. Most of the time, our cows knew when it was milking time, and we had no trouble getting them in the barn. But one afternoon, one cow decided she wanted to do something else and kept turning away from the barn and heading back to the pond, where she could wade in and cool off.

I tried everything to get her into the barn. I even used a five-gallon bucket of feed to entice her to go into the barn. Each time, she would act as if she was following me into the barn, but at the last moment, she would swing around and head in the other direction.

After about three times of refusing to go into the barn, I was getting mad. The next time she turned around, she stepped on my foot and nearly knocked me down. As a reflex, and without thinking, I swung the feed bucket at her head. I missed her head, but the bottom rim of the bucket hit her neck about halfway between her head and her shoulders. She dropped like a rock and, for a few seconds, didn't move or flinch.

My whole life, which actually was pretty short at that time, flashed before my eyes. I knew it would be hard to deny or explain how a healthy cow died while being milked.

But, after a few seconds, which seemed like hours to me, she rolled onto her belly, shook her head, and got up from the ground. She stood there for a minute or two, seemingly regaining her balance and then walked straight into the barn. I was able to milk her as if nothing had happened.

To this day, I do not know why she went down so fast. I had not hit her that hard, but there must be a vulnerable spot on a cow's neck. Apparently, the edge of the bucket hit that critical spot, temporarily stunning or paralyzing her, but otherwise she was fine. The next day, and to my relief, she was out in the pasture picking grass along with the other cows.

Although we kept three to five cows, we barely got enough milk for our needs. Our cows were always mixed heritage and didn't produce milk such as Hosteen's and Jerseys. Also, one or two of them would usually be dry or nursing a calf.

We always raised our own milk cows from calves born on our farm. Sometimes, the heritage of our calves wasn't planned but was the result of the particular bull we happened to have or which neighbor's bull broke through the fence first when the cow was in heat.

Dad selected our replacement cows by making a best guess at which heifer calf to keep rather than sell. He always tried to pick one that was most likely to produce a marketable calf and also give at least a half-gallon of milk.

Occasionally, and in the early spring, one or more of the cows would find a wild onion patch and help themselves. That would completely ruin the milk. No matter how badly we needed the milk, we could not stand the smell and taste of the wild onions in the milk. I figured they did that on purpose to get back at us for making them stay in our field and not allowing them to roam and find better grass. We would usually give the milk to the hogs, as they didn't seem to mind the wild onion flavor.

A neighbor lady loved wild onions and would always take the milk when asked. She would eat wild onions with her meals and sometimes by themselves. You didn't want to be within ten feet of her if she had been eating the onions.

We usually had a cat or two that hung around the barn, and we would sometimes squirt milk at them so we could watch them try to catch and drink it. I believe that was the main rea-son we occasionally had less milk than usual, and Mom would wonder what happened. She would ask if we were really sure that we had completely finished milking all the cows.

We never butchered a cow or calf while I was growing up. We always sold the calves and occasionally one of the cows if they were not giving enough milk. Our meat was always from hogs, and I am not sure I even knew people ate beef. A prime 400-pound calf, in 1950, would bring 25 cents per pound. The price now is around $5 per pound.

It was always exciting when we were ready to sell one of our animals. A local grocery store owner also operated a one-truck hauling service for delivering livestock to the Louisville Livestock Market. Dad would contact him when he wanted him to pick up an animal and take it to market.

He would come by on the day of the sale and pick up the animal we were selling. He always came way before daylight because he was picking up additional livestock from other farms and then had to make the 60-mile trip to Louisville. Get-ting up in the dark and watching or helping load the animal to be sold was interesting.

If we were selling a cow, we would always lock her in the barn the evening before, so we wouldn't have to chase her around the field the next morning and in the dark. We used lanterns for light and a bucket of feed to encourage her to climb the ramp to the truck. Sometimes, even with feed, she wouldn't want to go up the ramp, and we would have to try pushing and pulling her up and into the truck.

If we still couldn't get her into the truck, the hauler would use a shock stick. Even though I didn't like shock sticks, sometimes there was just no other way to get the animal loaded, especially when it was a bull that was trying to fight us. We were lucky and never got seriously hurt, but many people were injured while working with large livestock.

Over the Waterfall without a Barrel

My favorite place was the Rock House and the surrounding area, including the creek and rock cliffs. There was so much for young boys to do there. You could, for instance, swing on wild grape vines, walk on fallen trees across ditches, fish, camp, and search for arrowheads.

One day, my cousin Leroy and I were exploring around a fast-flowing spring that came out of the side of a hill near the Rock House. As soon as the stream of water left the spring, it followed a steep slope for about 50 feet. It then went beneath a rock overhang that was only a foot above the stream, making it look like a small tunnel, before going over a waterfall that was around ten feet high. After going over the falls, the water splashed onto large jagged rocks that covered the ground at the bottom of the waterfall. The stream then continued down the hill until it reached the creek that flowed in front of the Rock House.

The stream bed above the waterfall was flat rock and extremely slick with moss growing in it. The water was only an inch or two deep, and you could walk across it if you picked a fairly level spot close to the spring and were very careful on the slick rocks. But, if you did slip and fall, there was nothing to grab onto – not even a small bush.

I still remember the shock we would get when we first stepped into that cold spring water on our bare feet. But, it didn't take long for the shock to die down and the fast-flowing water to start feeling so good after a blistering hot summer day of climbing around on the cliffs.

Leroy and I had decided to chance walking across the stream of water instead of having to climb up the steep hill to go around the spring. While crossing the stream, I had stopped to take a drink by using my cupped hands to dip up the water.

I heard Leroy yell and then looked up and saw him sliding down the steep stream of water. He was on his back, going really fast, and feet first toward the waterfall. He tried to grab onto the overhanging rock ledge as he went under it, but was going too fast. He came out the other side of the overhang and then shot over the waterfall. After he went over the edge of the falls, I could no longer see him, but was able to hear him at the bottom yelling, "I'm killed".

It took me about ten minutes to get down to him because of the steepness of the hill and the sharp drop-offs. All that time, he kept yelling that he had been killed. I tried to assure him that if he were totally killed, he wouldn't be yelling.

While trying to make my way down to him, I kept thinking that if he was really killed, then I was going to have to do a lot of explaining. Everyone would want to know why we were in such a dangerous place to begin with and why we didn't know better than to try walking across those slick rocks.

But when I finally reached him, I was relieved that he wasn't killed, but his head was bleeding badly. He was just sitting on a big rock with the water still splashing all over him.

After a few minutes, his head stopped bleeding, and we washed off all the blood by holding his head under the falling water. Neither of us had on shirts, and his back looked as if some cat had been sharpening its claws on it. His pants were torn, and he was bruised and had a few small cuts on his hands, but we both knew it could have been much worse.

After about 15 minutes, even though he looked like a drowned cat, he felt ok to keep exploring. It was such a pretty day, neither of us wanted to give up and go home.

Shortly, we were laughing and talking about the great, free, and speedy thrill ride he had going over the waterfall.

According to him, it was sort of fun, but I never saw him step on those slick spots again. From then on, every time we went that direction to the Rock House, he would suggest that we should climb the hill and not walk through the spring water – it was too cold for our bare feet.

32

In the Interest of Science

I was always interested in how things worked, which was not necessarily a good thing, and often landed me in trouble. I was fascinated by firecrackers and often searched for uses other than just making a loud noise.

Getting up for school was always hard for me, especially in winter when I was buried under a pile of quilts. I would listen to the alarm clock until it wound down and then go back to sleep. I needed more motivation to get out of bed, and decided to build an explosive alarm clock.

I tried many different ways to build one and finally got a setup that occasionally worked the way I wanted. That model used a regular clock that had a small wind-up knob that turned when the clock was alarming.

When the clock began alarming, it would wind up a short string. If not turned off within a few seconds, the string would shorten, causing a spring-loaded match holder to scrape along a piece of sandpaper – hopefully lighting both the match and the firecracker.

As soon as I heard the alarm clock, I would need to jump out of bed and quickly shut it off, or else the firecracker would light and explode in our bedroom.

It would definitely not be good to let a firecracker go off in our bedroom at that time of morning. I was pretty sure I would be in trouble.

I kept improving the contraption and almost had it perfected, but eventually came to my senses and abandoned the whole effort. That most likely prevented me from burning the house down, or at a minimum, from being beaten up by my brothers.

Another time, I wondered what would happen if a firecracker exploded while underwater. I believed it should at least create small waves in the water. I also thought I might be able to see the waves if I was real close and looking directly at the top of the water.

Plastic pill bottles had just become available and seemed perfect for use in running an experiment. I decided to explode a firecracker at the very bottom of a bucket of water and see what happened. I practiced lighting firecrackers in plastic bottles, then quickly putting the bottle cap back on. After a couple of successful attempts, I decided I was ready to try it underwater.

I suspected I should try this outside the house, rather than inside, but Mom and everyone else were outside. This gave me time to conduct my experiment without having observers or grown-ups possibly questioning what I was doing. Besides, what could go wrong? The firecracker would be underwater, so no one should be able to hear it.

I set a bucket of water in the middle of the kitchen floor and tied the pill bottle to a small rock so it would sink quickly to the bottom of the bucket. After lighting the firecracker, I dropped the bottle in the bucket of water and leaned over it with my face about a foot above the water. I was hoping to see at least a few small ripples on top of the water when the firecracker went off.

The next thing I knew, I was knocked hard against the kitchen wall and soaked from head to toe. I couldn't see or hear well for a while, and water was dripping from everything in the kitchen, including the ceiling, stove, tables, and all four walls. Less than an inch of water remained in the bucket.

It didn't take but maybe half a second for Mom to show up, and for what seemed to me a long time, just stood there looking back and forth at the kitchen and me. I believe she was trying to decide which to do first - clean the kitchen or kill me.

I seemed to hear her counting under her breath, but she finally asked if I was okay and immediately began cleaning up the mess. She didn't fuss at me or even threaten me. It was almost as if she had been expecting something like this to happen and was glad it was over with.

Since this was before we had electricity, there was no danger of the water shorting out light fixtures or outlets. Most of the water was fairly easy to clean up with mops and old towels, and the rest was left to dry on its own. However, there were small bits of paper from the firecracker, most of them less than an eighth of an inch, pasted all over the ceiling. I couldn't believe just one firecracker contained that much paper.

We were able to clean most of the paper off the ceiling by sweeping it with the broom after it had dried. But some remained there for years. Mom may actually have left some of the paper on the ceiling as a reminder not to do that again.

After realizing Mom may not kill me, at least not yet, I did wonder if I had stumbled upon a quick way to wash the insides of barrels. A well-controlled water explosion should knock all dirt and other contaminants loose, making it easy to rinse them out. But, there would have to be some way to do it without all the firecracker paper. I intended to experiment with my new idea, but soon moved on to something else and forgot all about it.

I still feel a little guilty about an experiment I conducted using my Cousin Leroy as a Guinea pig. Our neighbor had an electric fence, and every time we were near it, we would dare each other to touch it. We would touch it with a green weed, and it would still hurt, but less than when we touched the wire with our bare hands.

I'm not sure how it got started, but we were trying different materials, such as pieces of dry and damp sticks and rocks, just to see which ones would or would not shock us.

Our electric fence experiments advanced to the point that I wanted to know if someone could pee on the wire without being shocked. I lied to Leroy and told him that I was sure that it would not shock anyone.

I am not sure of the exact details of my lie; however, I confidently gave him a bunch of made-up rationale, including that everyone knows electricity can't follow a stream of just water – it needs a wire or other material, such as weeds. Otherwise, all electric wires would be shorted out when it rained. That should have been a clue to him, because we and most other rural homes didn't even have electricity, and he should have asked where I got so much information about it. I further explained that pee would either completely block the electric or such a small amount would get through that it would be hard to feel it.

I still can't believe it, but he also became interested in knowing if that was really true and questioned me on how sure I was that it wouldn't shock him if he tried it. I gave him as good an answer as I could for someone who had never been around electricity nor had any idea of how it worked.

Even thinking about trying it himself was completely out of character for him, because usually, he would have told me that if I was so sure, then try it myself. I now believe he was so anxious to prove me wrong that he completely forgot about suggesting I try it first.

After I again assured him that I was absolutely positive there was no way it would shock him-he did it.

Based on his loud gasp and huge backwards jump, I quickly surmised that it really would shock you, and that our friendship was about to take an instant nosedive. I was right, and even though I was ready for it, he still got in at least one good punch before I was able to get away from him.

I am sure that was not true, but at the time, I thought I saw smoke come from his ears from either being nearly electrocuted or from being so mad.

I wanted to ask him how it felt, but I figured it would be better just to drop the subject – or as rural folks would often say, "let sleeping dogs lie".

We never mentioned the incident to each other again - I was afraid too, and he was probably too embarrassed about falling for the obvious lie.

Not that I blame him, but for a long time after that, he questioned nearly everything I told him.

33

Automobiles Then and Now

Essentially, all cars before the 1950s had standard stick-shifts, six rather than 12-volt batteries, and generators rather than alternators. One could almost tell which cars had weak batteries or were hard to start by observing where and how drivers parked their cars before turning them off.

If one's battery was low or if it was difficult to start the car while hot, it was always a good idea to park the car facing downhill, and with nothing blocking the path forward. By parking that way, a driver could, by themselves, get the car slowly rolling, jump in, and then start the car by letting out on the clutch while the car was in first or second gear.

Everyone occasionally had starting problems and needed help. It was not unusual to see two or three people helping someone push their car to get it started.

It was also easy to recognize less experienced drivers as they learned to correctly operate the clutch and change gears without grinding the transmission. Even experienced drivers sometimes were embarrassed if they inadvertently "ground" the transmission while changing gears.

Beginning in the 1960s, the use of 12-volt batteries and alternators instead of less efficient generators really improved the starting reliability of most cars. Alternators provided greater charging output, especially at lower engine speeds. The change was driven partly by the growing electrical demand of cars—brighter headlights, radios, power accessories, and later air conditioning—which generators were incapable of supporting.

In addition to stick-shift transmissions, all cars back then used carburetors to feed fuel to the engines and coils, breaker points, and spark plugs to create the spark for ignition. Most drivers spent considerable time tinkering with the carburetors, cleaning spark plugs, and adjusting the engine timing, trying to improve engine performance, including idling.

Mainly due to engine problems, many engines would die while idling, but sometimes the driver caused it to die by engaging the clutch too fast. In either case, the engine would have to be restarted. That could be a real problem if the battery were weak or you were on an upward incline with other cars close behind.

Back then, starter switches were foot-operated, and there was no park position on the transmission. You really needed three feet to restart the car without it rolling backwards and possibly hitting the car behind you. You needed one foot on the brake, one on the gas pedal, and a third to push the starter switch.

To prevent the car from dying in the first place, it was a common practice to shift the transmission to neutral while keeping the left foot on the brake and the right foot on the gas pedal.

When ready to start driving forward again, one had to shift the transmission to first gear by first lifting the foot off the brake and then using that foot to disengage the clutch pedal, while at the same time depressing the gas pedal. All of those actions had to be done as quickly as possible to minimize the car rollback distance after taking your foot off the brake.

Experienced drivers would always stop their car well behind the one in front of them, especially when they were stopping on an incline. They knew that the car in front would roll backwards, at least a short distance, when preparing to move forward.

Even today, with automatic transmissions and cars that seldom die when idling, it makes me nervous, and a little irritated, when I am stopped on an incline and other drivers pull up really close behind me. I always think they would soon learn not to do that if they pulled up that close behind someone driving a car with a stick-shift transmission.

I, as do most people who drove cars during the 1940s and 50s, still leave plenty of room between my car and the one in front.

I also still have a habit of using my left foot for braking and my right foot for operating the gas pedal - a carryover from those long-ago days.

Cars in the 1940s and 50's had no seat belts, child car seats, or electric turn signals. Just a few years ago, I had to add turn signals to an antique car, although they weren't required. Other drivers often mistook my hand signal for a friendly wave and just waved back instead of understanding that I was signaling a turn.

Another big change since back then is the level of service provided at service stations. When pulling into a service station in the 1940s and '50s, you actually received service. The attendant would rush out to pump your gas, check engine oil, clean your windshield, and check tire air pressure. If you asked, he would also remove the radiator cap and check the radiator coolant level.

We now seldom even refer to them as service stations. The name gas station is a much better description of how they operate today.

One could crank the engine by hand to start most cars built before the 1940s. However, most of those cars were prone to kickback, especially if the spark was not retarded before cranking the engine. Many a thumb and a few wrists were broken by not paying attention and allowing the thumb to wrap around the crank handle while starting the engine.

34

We Managed Without Insurance

In the 1940s, there were few government safety nets for rural families hit by disaster. A county welfare office or the Red Cross might provide temporary food, clothing, or even limited shelter, but rebuilding a burned house usually depended on neighbors, relatives, and church members coming together to help. Community was often the only real support a farm family could count on because most, including us, had no traditional insurance of any kind– not health or liability nor property.

Actually, there was less need for insurance back then because lawsuits from accidents were almost unheard of, medical costs were much lower than today, and neighbors were quick to help out if someone had a significant loss.

The fact that close kinship families lived near each other provided a level of insurance against catastrophes. We had my grandparents, Ma and Pa. If anything bad happened to our house, we could temporarily move in with them and vice versa.

A good thing about having country roads and older cars was that vehicle accidents were less frequent, and those that did happen tended to be fender benders rather than high-speed collisions.

If there had been a car accident, whoever was at fault would usually apologize and offer to help repair or pay for any needed repairs to the other vehicle. Typically, they would also offer to help around the farm if the other person was injured and possibly needed temporary help.

In 1975, Kentucky began requiring everyone to have liability insurance for vehicles.

The cost of seeing a doctor or spending time in a hospital was a burden on rural residents but not so expensive as to drive them deep into debt. The charge for a routine house call by the doctor in the early 1940s was usually around $2 to $5, and hospital stays of three days were typically $20 to $30 total. That was still a lot of money for rural residents such as us, but most medical providers allowed patients to make installment payments, making the debt more manageable.

Inflation alone since the 1940s would increase the cost of the same three-day hospital stay to around $2,000 today. However, mostly driven by more advanced medical diagnostics and treatments, the costs of a routine three-day hospital stay are now $45,000.

Back then, we only sent for a doctor when there was no doubt someone was really sick or badly hurt. Seeing a doctor go to someone's home was even more unusual and attention-getting than seeing an ambulance with sirens and flashing lights today.

A few years ago, I was dismissed as a potential juror because of beliefs developed during childhood. The plaintiff's lawyers dismissed me from being on the jury because they were afraid I wouldn't agree to award money to someone just because they had been in an accident that was not their fault.

There had been a car accident, and someone had sustained minor injuries, causing them to miss work for a few days.

The injured person had filed a lawsuit seeking to collect money for pain and suffering as a result of the accident.

I was being questioned as a potential juror, and the injured person's lawyer asked me, "Will you agree to award compensation to the plaintiff if the jury determines that the other person was at fault for the accident?" I answered. "I really don't know at this point, because I don't yet know enough about the specifics of the accident." I went on to explain that I would likely agree to compensation if the at-fault person had been unreasonably or intentionally negligent. I further explained that I generally believed a person at fault in an accident didn't necessarily owe the other person money, but should, as a minimum, apologize, and ensure the injured person was adequately compensated for lost wages and expenses.

Two other prospective jurors answered the same question by saying they agreed with me. Needless to say, neither of us three was selected as a juror.

I still sometimes wonder if I did the right thing by answering as I did. By us not being selected as jurors, the jury was essentially stacked with those who were comfortable awarding compensation based solely on who was at fault for the accident. But for me to say otherwise would have been untruthful.

We Finally Get Electricity

Around 1950, while living in Eastview, our home was finally wired for electricity. Initially, and for a couple of years, we used it solely for lighting – and what a difference it made.

Everyone today has experienced electrical power outages of a few hours or maybe even a week or more. I am sure they can remember the relief and excitement they felt when the power finally came back on.

All of my family, including my parents and their parents, had lived our entire lives without electrical power, and now we could just flip a switch and instantly have bright light anywhere in the house.

Suddenly, we could easily read and do homework at night, Mom could finish patching our shirts and pants after it had cooled off in the evenings, and Dad didn't have to keep refilling lamps with coal oil.

At night, we didn't have to locate a lamp, check that it had coal oil, clean the globe, or light a piece of paper in the stove to light the lamp. We also didn't need to adjust and trim the lamp wick and put up with the smoke coming out of the top of the globe. When temporarily going to another room to get something, we didn't have to leave others in the dark by carrying the lamp with us. Also, Mom could better see to pick briars and splinters out of our feet and hands, and quickly check on us when we were sick at night.

We eventually replaced our battery-powered radio with an electric one. We were then able to listen to our favorite shows, such as the Grand Ole Opry, The Lone Ranger, and even the news, without worrying about running the battery down. Over time, we added other electrical conveniences, including a used refrigerator and, eventually, a black-and-white 17-inch Arvin TV.

Billy always liked to eat a bowl of cornbread and milk for supper. He remembers how much better his supper tasted when his milk came cold from the refrigerator.

Later, we were able to buy or trade for an electric fan. Mom used it to help cool the kitchen while canning garden vegetables, and Dad used it to help him sleep when he had to lie on the floor because of his back.

Almost immediately, electricity began making subtle changes in our lives, some good - and others not so good. Good things were that milk and other perishable foods lasted much longer in the refrigerator, and we didn't have to worry about accidentally dropping a coal oil lamp and burning the house down.

But now, our parents had new challenges, such as paying the monthly electrical bill and making sure we kids got plenty of sleep rather than trying to stay up all night watching TV or reading.

We were staying up later at night, so getting up the next morning became more difficult. That made it harder on Mom to get us up so we could get the milking done and ready for school on time. But she soon learned to make us turn everything off and get in bed at a reasonable time.

For many years, we read the electric meter ourselves - a common practice in rural areas at the time. The electric company would first send us a postage-paid card with a space to record our electric meter reading. We would check the meter, write down the numbers, and mail the card back to the company. Using the readings we provided, the electric company would then calculate our usage and send us the electric bill, which we paid by mailing them the amount we owed.

The postal service was getting a lot of business with all the mailings; however, postage stamps were only three cents in the early 1950s.

Before we had electricity, one of our hogs, actually our best sow, had a habit of digging under the woven wire fence around our hog lot and getting out. As soon as she got out, she would head for the garden and help herself to tomatoes, carrots, and at least two or three other vegetables. The real problem was that she would damage much more than she ate.

Mom would inspect the damage to the garden and swear that if Dad didn't do something to keep her in the hog lot, she was going to get the rifle and shoot that thing.

Dad didn't want to get rid of her because she was an excellent pig producer and took good care of each litter with very few infant pig deaths.

Dad would repair the fence the best he could, but in a few days, she would manage to get out again. This went on for months, seemingly as if the sow and Dad were in a contest competing against each other.

Shortly after we had electricity, Dad obtained an old electric fence charger and put an electric wire all the way around the bottom of the hog lot. He informed Mom that the problem of the sow getting out was finally solved once and for all.

A few days later, she was out again. Dad himself was now threatening to get the rifle and shoot her. For a while, he actually considered putting another wire around the hog lot and plugging it directly into the house electrical outlet. He finally decided not to do that because the hog lot was sometimes muddy, and the sow and possibly some of the other hogs might be electrocuted.

Dad decided to just put up with it a little longer and give her some time to get used to the electric wire, and maybe she would tire of it and quit on her own. Although the electric fence didn't stop her right away, it was causing her to get out less often as time went by.

We always knew when she was getting ready to try getting out. She knew the electricity was going to hurt, but she really wanted out. She would back off a few feet from the fence, start squealing, and then, while still squealing, run at the fence trying to crawl under or through it as quickly as possible. Occasionally, she would make it out of the lot, but most of the time she would have to give up and try another day.

About the time Dad decided she'd be the first to go when the weather turned cold enough for butchering, she finally gave up her escape attempts—just in time to save herself from becoming bacon. We decided she had convinced herself it wasn't worth the pain now that cold weather had arrived and garden vegetables were gone anyway.

36

Our First TV

In 1954, a family that we knew was the first within five miles to own a TV. At least twice, our whole family visited them solely to watch their TV. Before that, I had only seen a TV in a store window in E-town.

Shortly after those visits, Billy began talking about how neat it would be to own a TV ourselves, and I was immediately hooked on the idea. Dad and Mom had other critical funding priorities, such as keeping us in clothes and food, and couldn't spare money for a TV. But since we were eager to get one, Dad agreed that if we were willing to do most of the work and not give up, he would help us rent and tend a tobacco patch so we could raise the money to buy a TV.

I believe he agreed so readily because he had seen the TV, and he wanted one himself.

We knew it would take a long time, but we set our sights on getting the TV and immediately began planning to do it. We decided to rent and tend a tobacco patch from one of our neighbors. Doug and Juanita were still too young to be of any real help to us, but we were pretty sure we could get it done, although it would take us all spring, summer, and part of the next winter before we could sell the tobacco and buy the TV. Dad helped us with the really tough parts, such as increasing the size of his tobacco bed so we wouldn't have to construct one ourselves.

Dad actually helped much more than we were expecting. He began by getting the neighbor to agree to rent us his tobacco patch, then helped us prepare the ground and set out the young plants. He also helped with cutting, housing, and stripping the mature tobacco. We probably could have done all that ourselves, but it would have been much harder.

The farmer that we were renting from trusted us to follow through and do a good job with his tobacco. He made a major commitment by agreeing to furnish all materials we would need, such as fertilizer and insecticides, and we could pay him back from the money we received when the tobacco was sold.

After we set out the plants, we began worrying whether we were getting enough rain, just as adults did. We kept an eye on the tobacco patch all summer, making sure the tobacco plants were well hoed and weeds were cut or pulled as soon as they came up. That was probably the best-looking tobacco patch in the county.

Although we now had our own tobacco patch to tend, we also had to keep doing our other jobs, including helping with the home tobacco patch. That was a pretty busy summer, but it gave us the experience and reputation such that later, Billy and I each rented and tended a tobacco patch on our own. In all cases, the rest of the family helped us when we needed them.

One day, while we were working in our rented tobacco patch, a bad, fast-moving lightning storm suddenly appeared. We had no way to get back home ahead of the storm because we had walked the mile or so to the tobacco patch. We also had no shelter other than nearby trees. We ran under a large tree and stood close against the tree trunk, trying to stay as dry as we could. That gave a little protection from the blowing rain, but we were still completely soaked.

We didn't realize it at the time, but standing under and against that tree in an open field during a severe lightning storm was really dangerous. Lightning was crashing all around us, but luckily, the tree was not struck. In just a short while, the sun came back out and dried us off, and we went back to work.

The tobacco grew well, and in the early fall, we cut and hung it in the barn to cure. In early November, we stripped it, and Dad hauled it to market for us. Per our agreement, we gave 1/2 of the proceeds to the landowner and then paid him back for the materials he had provided.

Nearly a year after we had decided to get a TV, we finally had the money and couldn't wait to buy it. It turned out that our share of the tobacco profits was just the right amount to buy a used 17-inch black-and-white Arvin TV and an outdoor antenna.

The TV had one knob to select channels 2 through 13 and another knob for the volume control. At that time, all TVs and programming were in black and white, and the largest available TV screen was 21 inches. Transistors and integrated circuits had not been invented, so all TVs used electronic tubes for the circuitry and a Cathode Ray Tube for displaying the picture. The tubes required about 30 seconds to warm up after turning on the TV.

We were able to get all three Louisville stations by rotating the antenna to the midpoint of the three channels. All channels still had snow and interference, but the pictures were acceptable.

Programming included lots of westerns such as Gene Autry and Roy Rogers, horror movies, wrestling, and a short 15-minute national news program each afternoon at 5:30.

All TV stations shut down programming after about 10 PM and broadcast special test patterns for the rest of the night.

Color TVs, remote controls, transistors, LEDs, large screens, and more than three stations were not yet even a dream. But that didn't matter to us since TV itself was a new technology.

It didn't take long for word to get around that we had a TV, and occasionally, one or more neighbors would show up around dark, and after supper, to watch it with us until nearly bedtime.

It was understood that if someone had a TV, then everyone would be welcome to come in, sit down, and watch whatever program was on. No one ever asked for the channel to be changed, and like a movie theater, there was very little talking. Occasionally, when it was really hot, we would move the TV in front of an open window, and everyone would sit in the yard to watch it.

Everyone would quietly watch the TV except for this one neighbor who loved watching professional wrestling. When wrestling was on, he would really get into the show and get so worked up that he would keep moving closer to the TV while yelling and shaking his fist at the bad guy.

He would become so agitated, Mom became concerned he might forget it was not real and throw something at the TV.

Just to be sure, she began keeping things out of his reach while he watched the wrestling show.

There was a lot of discussion and even arguments among both kids and adults about whether wrestling was real or fake. About one-half of the people would swear it was real, and the other half would swear it was fake.

A few times, neighbors stayed so long that Dad was about ready to tell them to turn it off when they left because he needed to go to bed.

The national news program back then was 15 minutes long on all three stations. That was plenty long enough to summarize critical events and provide all the information we needed. It wasn't until 1963 that most stations increased the news programs to 30 minutes. Today, at least seven stations broadcast news "shows" 24 hours a day. Obviously, there aren't enough important news items to fill the 24 hours, so most stations now rely heavily on talk shows and "experts" simply stating opinions rather than facts to fill the time.

37

My University Experiences

I enrolled at the University of Kentucky and earned a degree in electrical engineering. When I first started, I had no idea what the cost would be—probably for the best, since knowing might have discouraged me from even trying. By working summers, borrowing through the student loan program, and with Mom and Dad contributing what they could, I managed to get through.

A big help in my decision to attend college was winning my high school's first-ever scholarship award program. It was actually an interest-free $500 loan to be repaid soon after graduation. The school's objective was to establish an ongoing program by loaning the repaid funds to another student. At that time, the $500 was nearly enough for the first year's tuition.

I repaid the loan during my first year out of college, though I'm not sure the program lasted much longer. It seemed the program must have been struggling just a couple of years after it began. One of my former teachers even asked if I would postpone my junior year to teach math at my high school, which would have allowed me to pay off the loan early, before graduation. I decided against it—I wanted to finish school as quickly as possible, and I worried that if I stepped away for a year, I might never go back.

I decided to go into electrical engineering because I enjoyed working with electronics, and I was much better at science and math than at less technical subjects, such as English and literature.

When I graduated from high school, I received all the math, science, and physics awards. I was also selected as the class valedictorian, but during my first semester at the University of Kentucky, I had to take a remedial, no-credit English subject.

During my senior year of high school, my classmates selected me as "Most Likely to Succeed". Years later, during my fortieth class reunion, I was voted "Most Changed". I don't know what the rationale was for the perceived big change and didn't dare ask.

I didn't have a car my first year at UK, so I hitchhiked a few times back and forth from home to school. Hitchhiking was always interesting and not too dangerous back then. Some drivers, instead of simply letting me out at their turnoff, would go out of their way and take me to a better spot to catch the next ride. Most of the time, I was able to get home by hitchhiking nearly as soon as I would have by driving.

I was feeling confident in my hitchhiking skills, so one day I decided to go to Mount Sterling, about 35 miles east of Lexington, to visit my aunt. I had no problem getting there, as I lucked out and caught a ride from someone going all the way through Mount Sterling. He dropped me off right at my aunt's door.

After visiting with my aunt and having dinner with her, I headed back to the UK. I had declined her offer to drive me back to school because I felt confident I would quickly catch a ride.

However, after walking about 10 miles and still without a ride, I started thinking I may have made a mistake by not accepting her offer. But just about the time I was giving up and deciding I was going to have to walk the entire 35 miles back to Lexington, I got a ride.

I remember he was an older gentleman who lived a few miles out of Lexington, toward Louisville. I guess he could tell I was tired from all the walking, and drove me all the way to my dorm. That hot walk broke me from hitchhiking, and after that, and for the rest of my freshman year, I only went home when I could find another student with a car and going that way.

Before my second year, my dad bought an old 1951 Chevrolet car and gave it to me. I made a few repairs so that I could use it to drive back and forth to the UK. However, I wasn't able to fix a leaky radiator and a small head gasket leak, both of which seemed fairly minor to me. I didn't mind refilling the radiator every time I drove it or seeing some steam from the leaking head gasket coming out of the car's tailpipe.

When driving, I often noticed that cars close behind me had their windshield wipers on even though it wasn't raining. There must have been more steam being thrown out of the tailpipe than I realized.

During my second year, I rented a small room (or closet) from an elderly lady on a dead-end street about a block off Rose Street and only a few blocks from many of the engineering buildings. I used her kitchen and lived mostly on chicken noodle soup.

What I remember most about my landlady was how she would back out of her driveway onto the side street. She would put the car into reverse, blow her horn, and take off backwards.

Luckily, her driveway was at least 50 feet long, so pedestrians and cars had about five seconds to get out of the way or get run over. It was actually funny to watch locals check her driveway before walking or driving past it.

Every time I heard that horn, I would listen for a crash. But I lived there for a full year and never knew of her hitting anyone or anything. I believe she thought there was something in the driver's manual that said anything goes as long as you blow your horn.

While living there, I had an opportunity to talk with Senator John Kennedy when he was a candidate for President, but I passed it up. I was walking to class down Rose Street, and Kennedy was in a convertible being driven in the opposite direction. Apparently, he had been campaigning somewhere on

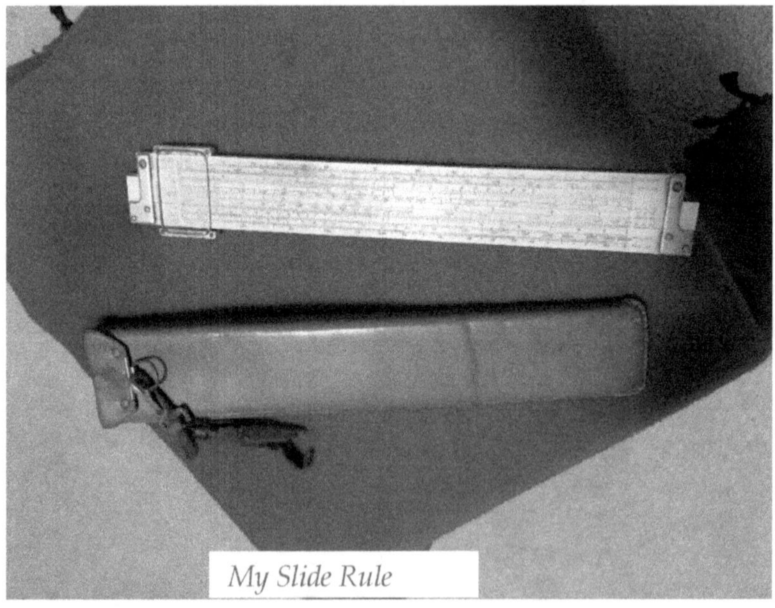

My Slide Rule

campus. There were no other vehicles in sight, and I was the only person on the street. He slowed down, waved at me, and started pulling over to the curb as if he wanted to talk to me or ask a question. However, at the time, I was already late for class and didn't want to risk being even later, so I just waved back at him and went on. .

As one walked across campus, engineering students were easy to spot—they were the ones with a slide rule hanging from their belt. Pocket calculators weren't yet available, making slide rules an essential tool for every engineering student. I relied on mine throughout college and for a few years after graduation. Though the answers were not exact, a slide rule could provide very accurate approximations, which, most of the time, are good enough. I still have mine, but these days, I'd probably struggle to multiply two times four with it.

During my third year, a friend and I shared a room on Grosvenor Avenue that included the entire upstairs, thus saving each of us quite a bit of money. The landlady also allowed us to use the kitchen.

Just about the time we were ready to move in, the university decided that all junior year students must live in a dorm. Apparently, they had just opened several new dorms that were not fully occupied. I met with the administration personnel and convinced them that if I had to move to a dorm, I would either have to leave school or go without food for the whole year. I could not afford the cost of living in the dorm and eating meals in the cafeteria. They gave me an exception to the new dorm policy, and my roommate and I lived in the apartment for the remainder of my time at UK.

Soon after we moved in, someone directly across the street got two large dogs that would lie on the bank about five feet above and facing the street. Every time my roommate or I would be walking to or from school, the dogs would bark and fake-charge us as if they were going to cross the street and attack us. We were actually concerned that they would.

Also, the almost constant barking directly across from our upstairs apartment window was interfering with our studies. Asking the owner several times to control the dogs did no good.

One night, the dogs were lying on the bank barking and threatening those passing by. We had a few firecrackers and decided to scare the dogs, but not actually hurt them. We bundled two or three firecrackers together and then tied the bundle to a small rock. As usual, and as soon as we stepped outside, the dogs started barking and growling at us. We lit the firecrackers and threw the bundle high in the air across the street and toward the dogs.

I could still draw an accurate picture of the glowing fuses as they sailed up and over the street in a perfect arc. I guess it was the luck of the first throw, but the rock went between the two dogs as they stood about two feet apart, and the firecrackers went off exactly at their eye level. The explosion was so loud, it actually echoed up and down the street.

Each dog took off in a different direction and fast. A few minutes later, and after we had gone back inside, we heard the owner softly whistling for his dogs. We believed he thought they had been shot as the firecrackers sounded exceptionally loud on the quiet, dark street. We were never bothered by the dogs again, and I don't even remember ever seeing them again.

The owner must have been keeping them up and only letting them out late at night, or else got rid of them.

I also recall a few other things that happened while we were renting on Grosvenor Avenue. One I will never forget, even if my head fell off.

Our landlady would occasionally ask my roommate and me to have dinner with her and her friends or family. She was a good cook, and we always looked forward to eating real food. Tea was always served from a big, heavy glass pitcher that was given to her by her grandmother. She often mentioned how much she treasured that pitcher. It must have been old, since she was quite old herself.

One day, my roommate and I were in the kitchen fixing something to eat. I needed some boiling water, so I heated it in a pan and then poured it into the pitcher. When I picked up the pitcher, the whole bottom came off in one piece. It was a perfectly smooth break all the way around the pitcher.

My whole life flashed before my eyes as I would rather take a beating than have to tell her I had broken her pitcher. Out of desperation, I used Elmer's glue and glued the bottom back on, hoping it would hold long enough for her to use it and maybe think it just broke from old age. The break was so clean, I couldn't even see it after gluing it back together, and thankfully, it didn't leak.

It did hold, and she continued to use it to serve tea at dinners. However, I never enjoyed another meal there as I was a complete nervous wreck when anyone picked up the pitcher and passed it across the table. I couldn't imagine the mess it would make if it came apart, allowing the bottom and all the tea to fall and smash onto the table and the food. When asked if I wanted tea, I would always say, "Thanks, but I am trying to drink more water." I wanted the pitcher anywhere but near me when the bottom fell off.

I came close to confessing several times, but never got up the courage. The glue was still holding when I graduated at least a year later, and may still be to this day.

While I was in the UK, Adolph Rupp, known for his temper, was the head basketball coach. One day, my roommate drove me over to Memorial Coliseum to get something out of my locker. As we pulled up, we saw Rupp leaving and decided it would be safe to park in his personal parking spot since it was right by the door, and we would only be there for a few minutes anyway. We were wrong. When we came out, Rupp was parked right behind us, blocking us in.

Apparently, he had forgotten something and returned to get it. It didn't take long for us to get the message that he was upset about someone, especially students, having the gall to park in his special reserved parking space.

I heard words from him that I had never heard before, and didn't even know existed. Actually, I believe he used up all the bad words he knew and then made up several more. We got his meaning, even if we didn't know what they meant. I was glad he was in a hurry and needed to leave, or we might still be there learning even harsher words.

My hardest class at UK turned out to be swimming, which I had been counting on to be my easiest. I had been swimming in ponds and creeks around home since I was about six years old. With that vast experience, I figured choosing swimming for my required physical education class would be a sure and easy "A." I considered myself a good swimmer and thought about signing up for the advanced class to show off my swimming skills. But I finally decided to take the easier route and signed up for the intermediate level class.

On day one, the instructor stated the minimum requirements for receiving a grade, and I immediately knew I was in trouble. The requirements included swimming the length of the swimming pool underwater, using a diving start from the highest diving board, which was at least 10 feet high. The diving board was three or four times higher than the highest creek bank I had ever jumped off. The pool was likely smaller than an Olympic pool, but it looked to be a quarter mile long to me.

It didn't take long for me to realize that my vast experience of having jumped a few times, feet-first, into the muddy waters of a shallow creek, and then dog paddling back to the bank, was not quite the same as what I now faced. I had never actually dived head-first because the creeks weren't deep enough, and often had logs and big rocks hidden just below the surface.

My cousin learned the hard way that jumping or diving into creeks, when you can't see the bottom, might not be wise. One afternoon, we were wading in a shallow creek looking for a place deep enough to swim, and he saw a small area that looked acceptable to him. Without first checking for logs or rocks, he just dived in and took off swimming with his head just below the surface. After a few feet, his head hit a large rock, and after standing up, blood was flowing from a one-inch gash on the top of his head.

The bleeding soon stopped, and we decided we had swum enough for that day. From then on, he was a little more careful about just diving in.

After a few painful belly busters into the university swimming pool, I was able to pretty much dive headfirst from the diving board. A better description of my dive might have been upper-body first. I had a hard time getting over the fear that a big rock might be hiding beneath the diving board.

I soon learned to remain underwater long enough, but couldn't make it to the other end of the pool because I kept veering off course and into the other lanes. Sometimes I would wind up swimming nearly crosswise across the pool. I couldn't understand how everyone else could swim in a straight line all the way from one end of the pool to the other.

The class instructor was watching me one day and asked if I was trying to swim with my eyes shut. That surprised me as I didn't know anyone could keep their eyes open underwater. Ponds and creeks are usually dirty and muddy, and you didn't dare open your eyes underwater - even for a second. If you did, somebody would likely have to lead you home.

I then began practicing opening my eyes underwater and finally mastered it. I had a difficult time doing it because I was so used to making sure I didn't open my eyes. What a difference it made! On my very next attempt, I easily followed my lane and made it to the other end of the pool. The straight line was actually the shortest distance I had been swimming underwater in weeks.

After a long, hard semester of trying to learn the required strokes, I passed the course with a grade of "C" and was glad I hadn't signed up for the advanced class.

38

My First Jobs

Although Billy and I were often busy in Dad's tobacco patch, we did occasionally have time to work for neighbors and earn some money of our own. I was about 12 years old the first time I worked for a neighbor, helping to set out their tobacco patch. Some jobs, such as setting out tobacco plants, could be completed more easily and faster by youngsters like myself, as they involve a lot of almost continuous bending over to the ground, which could be difficult for some adults.

We weren't able to help others very much because all tobacco crops tended to be on the same general work schedules. Farmers needed to get their tobacco set out as soon as possible after the threat of frost was over – usually the first two weeks of May. That meant that everyone, including us, was busy at the same time setting out their own tobacco and was not available to help others.

The same was true for other labor-intensive jobs associated with the tobacco crops, including cutting, housing, and stripping the tobacco.

When neighbors were desperate for help, they would offer to pay as much as $3 a day. That now seems low, but it actually was pretty good pay, as most things at that time were much cheaper than now. Gas was 29 cents a gallon.

Between my Junior and Senior years in High School, I rented a tobacco patch from a neighbor so I could make some money for my first year of college. Billy was working in Indiana and so was not available to help me.

Raising that tobacco turned out to be much more work than I was expecting. For some reason, the owner wanted to move the tobacco patch from its usual location near the barn to a new location within the pasture.

Placing the tobacco patch in what had just recently been a pasture made it extremely difficult to control the grass and weeds and prevent them from taking over.

I fought weeds with plows and hoes all summer long. Finally, the tobacco was sold, and I was surprised it did as well as it did.

My first job that involved a real paycheck was with Tyler Construction Company of Louisville, Ky. I worked for them for one summer between my sophomore and Junior years in college (1960). My dad was then the Superintendent of a work crew constructing many of the concrete streets in and around Louisville.

My job was to interpret the design drawings and install guides along the edge of the street, so other workers knew where and how to set the forms for pouring the concrete. If the forms were not set correctly, the concrete street would be at the wrong height or width.

This was pretty straightforward work except when streets intersected each other or involved banked curves. Then I had to be really careful in making sure the crew setting the forms knew what was required.

I had only one real problem all summer, but it was a big one. I had placed strings outlining the height of the street that was to be poured as it intersected another street. Visually, it looked too high, so I checked and rechecked the drawings to be sure I was calculating everything correctly.

However, the guys setting the forms allowed that I must have figured it wrong, as the new street would be at least three inches higher than the existing intersecting street.

I tried but couldn't convince them I was right, and so they set the forms to match the existing street level and poured the intersection three inches lower than the design drawings. The next day, the city inspector came out to approve the work, but said it was all wrong and that we would have to remove and redo the entire intersection.

We had to tear out the intersection, haul off the recently poured concrete, and pour the whole thing again. That took at least three days and about 10 large truckloads of concrete.

The city had been getting ready to redo the intersecting street and planned to make it higher than the current one to get better water drainage. Neither I nor any of the work crew knew about the long-term plan.

Although not directly my fault, thinking back on this, I should have insisted on contacting the city inspector to get clarification before proceeding. But I was young and new to the job, and these guys had worked these streets for years, so I didn't push it and went along with their decision. The good thing was that they didn't question me again all summer.

The other thing I will never forget was when I thought I was about to be killed by a road grader. I was all by myself, sitting on the bare ground of a graded dirt street at the bottom of a small hill. I was intensely studying the drawings and trying to figure out how the concrete was supposed to be sloped as it reached the very bottom of the hill and started up the other side. I didn't know anyone was within a mile of me.

All of a sudden, I heard a loud horn, and someone yelled behind me. When I looked around, the front wheel of a large road grader was about three inches from my back. Front wheels on graders are huge, about five feet tall. Since I was sitting on the ground, the wheel looked to be at least 10 feet tall.

I jumped at least six feet straight up from a sitting position. I didn't know anyone or anything, except a frog, could jump straight up from a sitting position, but I apparently did. Then I heard the grader operator laughing his head off.

He had turned off his engine and let the grader roll silently down the hill of the dirt road and right up against my back before stopping it and blowing his horn. He could tell I was too busy to notice the grader creeping up on me.

It is funny now, but not quite as funny then. Of course, I pretended to know the grader was coming toward me and that it didn't scare me. But I wasn't too believable since my sunburned face was white as a sheet and my heart was pounding so hard the front of my shirt was actually flapping.

The design drawings had been scattered all over the road, and my pencil, notebook, and other items had been thrown about 20 feet, some on top of the road bank. But I still insisted it didn't scare me.

I only worked in Louisville that one summer because the next summer, between my Junior and Senior years, I applied for and was selected for a summer engineering job at the Air

Force's Aerospace Test and Evaluation Center located in Tullahoma, Tennessee.

During the 12 weeks I worked in Tennessee, I made at least three trips back to Kentucky to see my future wife, Faye. She was working at a pharmaceutical distribution center on Broadway in Louisville and staying at her sister's home.

Those trips to Louisville weren't all that easy before interstates were built, and in an old car that wouldn't start while hot. I had to keep it running even while getting gas.

Most of the time, I didn't leave Louisville, heading back to Tullahoma, before around midnight. I would get one or two hours of sleep and then have to get up and head to work.

The summer job worked out really well, and after graduation, I was offered and accepted a full-time engineering job at the Aerospace Test Center.

39

My Wife Faye and Her Family

Faye is the daughter of Clyde and Thelma Hay, who resided near Big Clifty, Kentucky, and is the second youngest of six girls and one boy. There was a 20-year age difference among her siblings. Her four older sisters were either married or soon to be by the time she was five or six.

Faye grew up the way I did – on a small family farm in Central Kentucky without electricity or indoor plumbing. They also used wood stoves for heating their home and for cooking.

Just as we did, her family grew tobacco as their primary cash crop. Also like us, they raised a few head of cattle for milk and to produce calves to sell. They raised a large garden and tended hay and corn crops as feed for their livestock.

Since there were six girls and only one boy in Faye's family, the girls had to help with the many farming tasks, such as working in the tobacco patch and caring for the animals.

While her older sisters were still at home, Faye didn't have to do much outside the home. Being much younger, she was often assigned to watch the food cooking on the wood stove while her Mom was working outside in the garden or field.

Faye loved to read, and before going outside, her Mom would often admonish her to every once in a while, put down the book and make sure the food didn't burn.

Faye had to work in the tobacco patch after her older sisters married and left home. As I did at her age, she helped with most tasks associated with raising the tobacco crop, from setting out the young plants to stripping the cured stalks. About the only thing she didn't do was climb into the top of the barn to hang the tobacco.

Faye's Mom & Dad with Left to Right - Faye; Betty; Lela; Pauline; Cecil; Dorothy; Barbara - Around 1959

I, at first, hardly noticed Faye because she was three years younger than me and a sixth-grader while I was a freshman in High School. However, when I was a senior in high school, I began noticing that, although she was only a freshman, she was really smart and very pretty.

We started dating while she was a sophomore in High School and I was a freshman at the University of Kentucky. We were married soon after I graduated in 1962 and have two children: Sandra and Glenn.

Our Family - Faye, Glenn, Sandra, Me - 1977

Afterword

The 1940s and 50s were the beginning of the end for small subsistence farms like ours, and the way that my siblings and I grew up.

Tractors were replacing horses during the late 1940s, and at the same time, many small farms were being merged into larger farming enterprises.

During the 1950s, life-changing technologies were being developed and introduced at a rapid pace. Orbital satellites, lasers, optical fibers, solar cells, transistors, and integrated circuitry were all becoming commonplace, and affecting the way people lived, communicated, and worked. These and numerous other inventions enabled the later development of modern conveniences, such as color TVs, cell phones, dishwashers, computers, and microwave ovens.

Within a very few years, the country went from kids, including me, walking barefoot to a one-room school, 3-transistor radios being the must-have item, and small grocery stores within every few miles to men walking on the moon and cell phones with billions of transistors and capable of communicating worldwide.

The photo of my brother Billy and my Dad using a tractor in the 1960s to pull the very same plow that just a few years earlier, during my childhood, had been pulled by our horses symbolizes the progress toward a completely different way of life.

Dad and Billy Using a Tractor to Pull a Horse-Drawn Plow

Our family began the transition away from farming during the late 1950s. At that time, Dad started working for a road construction firm in Louisville to supplement his farming income. In the 1960s, he gave up farming as his primary income and worked full-time as the superintendent of a street-building crew.

Mom continued doing what she always did – mostly worrying about us, even though we were grown, had left the nest, and were bringing her grandkids to both enjoy and worry about. Billy completed a self-study course in electronics and

Mom and Dad in 1990

Billy at the TV Station Console

opened a TV repair shop, installed satellite TV systems, and operated and maintained a local TV station. Doug attended a community college in Campbellsville, Kentucky, and became a skilled machine operator. He retired from Navistar in

Springfield, Ohio, and spent quality time enjoying his many grandchildren.

Doug Playing with Grandkids

Juanita graduated from the University of Louisville and managed her husband's dental office in Benton, Kentucky. She is now retired and loves to travel with her expanding family.

Juanita and Husband Jerry on Travel

It was June 16, 1962, and I was at home in Big Clifty, Kentucky, sitting in my 1959 Ford car that I had bought on credit just a week earlier. I had driven to the end of our lane and stopped to look back at the home where I had grown up and now was leaving

Two weeks earlier, I had graduated from the University of Kentucky with an electrical engineering degree, and was now on my way to a local church to be married. Immediately after the ceremony, my bride and I planned to leave for my new job and a new life in Tennessee.

As I looked back up the lane to our house, I knew this was the end of one journey and the beginning of another. I recalled the nights I had lain on my back in the yard, hoping to see a falling star just as it began to fall. I remembered the day we got electricity and how thrilling it was to flip a switch and immediately have a bright light. I also recalled getting our first TV and how our knowledge of places and events, all over the world, suddenly expanded a thousand fold. I knew I would never forget the good and the not-so-good times we had at our one-room school and the friendships that would last a lifetime.

Now, in just a few days, I would begin helping achieve President Kennedy's goal of landing a man on the moon before the end of the decade. I didn't know it at the time, but I would have a diverse and fulfilling career that would include managing operations of the world's largest and most complex space and propulsion test facilities. Later, I would support contract operations at NASA, Air Force, and Navy aeronautical, space, and defense-related sites, including Cape Kennedy,

Houston, White Sands, Stennis, and Langley and Ames Research Centers.

I Am Standing and Discussing the Prototype System I Designed and Developed to Improve Jet Engine Safety

It could have been a sad moment, but as I drove away, the excitement of turning a new page in my life completely canceled out all negative thoughts.

I do not regret growing up the way I did and would do it again in a heartbeat. Our simplistic, but hard, rural way of life taught us responsibility, patience, and care for family and community.

Acknowledgement

My utmost gratitude to my brother Billy and my sister Juanita, whose generous help in recalling events, places, and moments brought these memories back to life.

And especially thanks to my wife Faye for putting up with me all these years.

Author Bio

Rooted in generations of Appalachian heritage, I grew up on small subsistence farms in central Kentucky during the 1940s and '50s — in a world without electricity or indoor plumbing, where children went barefoot as long as the weather permitted and worked alongside their parents from an early age. We lived off the land, attended a one-room schoolhouse, crafted our own toys, and used horses to plow and tend the crops, including the family's burley tobacco patch. Those early years taught me perseverance, responsibility, faith, and resourcefulness — lessons that shaped the course of my life.

After earning a degree in electrical engineering from the University of Kentucky, I spent my entire professional career supporting U.S. Air Force and NASA air and space programs. My work included contributions to military jet engine and ballistic missile system development, as well as the rocket motors that powered the Apollo program lunar landings.

I began my career as an instrumentation engineer at the Arnold Engineering Development Center (AEDC) in Tullahoma, TN in 1962 and retired from Jacobs Engineering Corporation in 2002 as Vice President and Deputy General Manager of the AEDC Group.

My life has spanned one of the most transformative periods in American history — from horsepower to rocket power. In these pages, I bring both firsthand experience and professional perspective to that extraordinary journey.

Faye and I live in Beechgrove, Tennessee.